Family Myths:
Psychotherapy Implications

Family Myths: Psychotherapy Implications

Stephen A. Anderson
Dennis A. Bagarozzi
Editors

Routledge
Taylor & Francis Group
New York   London

Family Myths: Psychotherapy Implications has also been published as *Journal of Psychotherapy & the Family*, Volume 4, Numbers 3/4 1988.

The Haworth Press, Inc., 12 West 32 Street, New York, NY 10001
EUROSPAN/Haworth, 3 Henrietta Street, London WC2E 8LU England

This edition by Routledge:

Routledge
Taylor and Francis Group
270 Madison Avenue
New York, NY 10016

Routledge
Taylor and Francis Group
2 Park Square, Milton Park
Abingdon, Oxon OX14 4RN

Library of Congress Catalogin-in-Publication Data

Family myths : psychotherapy implications / Stephen A. Anderson, Dennis A. Bagarozzi, guest editors.
    p. cm.
   Also published as Journal of psychotherapy & the family, vol. 4 nos. 3/4, 1988.
   Included bibliographical references.
   ISBN 0-86656-775-5
   1. Family psychotherapy. 2. Myth – Psychological aspects. 3. Family. I. Anderson, Stephen A. (Stephen Alan), 1948- . II. Bagarozzi, Dennis A.
RC488.5.F3254   1988
616.89'156 – dc19   88-30091
                                                          CIP

We would like to dedicate this volume to Dr. Antonio J. Ferreira, MD who died in May, 1986. Dr. Ferreira's seminal ideas on family myths have been the cornerstone for work in this area of family process and the contents of this volume in particular.

When we first began this project in January, 1986, we contacted Dr. Ferreira and asked him to author a paper for the collection. He declined because of poor health and because his interests had long since shifted from family psychiatry to marine biology. However, he was extremely gratified to learn that his concept of family myth was still adding to our understanding and handling of relationships. He also noted that had our invitation arrived at a different time, the excitement of the project "might have rekindled old fires." We sincerely wish that our timing had been better.

Family Myths:
Psychotherapy Implications

CONTENTS

ABOUT THE EDITORS

Stephen A. Anderson, PhD, is Director of the Marital and Family Therapy Training Program and Associate Professor at the University of Connecticut, School of Family Studies in Storrs, Connecticut. Dr. Anderson earned his doctorate degree in family and child development at Kansas State Universtiy and has been in clinical practice as a maritial and family therapist for over 15 years. In addition to being an editorial board member of the *Journal of Strategic and Systemic Therapies*, he is a reviewer for the *Journal of Marriage and the Family* and the *Journal of Social and Personal Relationships*. Dr. Anderson has written numerous articles for professional journals.

Dennis A. Bagarozzi, MSW, PhD, is a former university professor now in full time private practice in Atlanta, Georgia at the Alliance for Counseling and Therapeutic Services. Trained as a lay analyst in New York City and as a family therapist at the Albert Einstein College of Medicine, Bronx State Hospital, he is a Fellow of the American Psychological Association (Division of Family Psychology), and a Fellow and Approved Supervisor of the American Association for Marriage and Family Therapy. A prolific writer on individual, maritial, and family therapy, Dr. Bagarozzi serves on the editorial boards of numerous clinical and research journals and edits the Family Measurement Techniques Section of the *American Journal of Family Therapy*.

Drs. Anderson and Bagarozzi have been studying the role of myths in psychotherapy for over a decade.

EDITORIAL NOTE

The importance of family myths is well established. Yet theoretical work in this area as well as empirically verified clinical methods are clearly under developed. The editors are pleased to present this special collection focusing on the family myths.

The editors of this collection were faced with the mission of providing the practicing psychotherapist with a comprehensive array of well-written, accurate, authoritative and relevant information vital to working with clients about interpersonal and family-related issues. The essays presented here, with their concern with the integration of theory, research and treatment, fit this mission extremely well. The editors faced the challenge of identifying and illustrating the importance of family myths for effective psychotherapy practice. They have more than met the challenge and have delighted us in the undertaking.

All of the contributors to this collection have focused specifically on myths as a central feature of their written and clinical work. This outstanding, international group of authors represents numerous disciplines and theoretical perspectives of mythological systems. They were attracted to the project by the creative forces and proven abilities of the editorial efforts of Stephen Anderson and Dennis Bagarozzi.

Professor Anderson is Director of the University of Connecticut's

Marital and Family Therapy Training Program. Dr. Bagarozzi is a former member of the faculty of several universities and is now in private practice at the Alliance for Counseling and Therapeutic Services (ACTS) in Atlanta. Both editors have published widely on mythological systems. Their recent book, *Personal, Marital and Family Myths: Theoretical Formulations and Clinical Strategies* (Bagarozzi and Anderson, in press) will be published by W. W. Norton in the near future.

Family myths and their treatment are underutilized by family therapists, according to editors Anderson and Bagarozzi. Indeed, they suggest that family psychotherapists should attend much more to the symbolic and affective components of human relationships in helping families change in intended ways.

Charles R. Figley, PhD
Editor

Family Myths: An Introduction

Stephen A. Anderson
Dennis A. Bagarozzi

As many of the authors in this collection of papers attest, it was Antonio Ferreira (1963) who first coined the phrase, "family myth." He defined family myths as a series of well integrated beliefs which are shared by all family members. He postulated that these beliefs prescribe the complementary role relationships that all participants in the family are required to play vis à vis other family members. For Ferreira, the family myth was thought to be the focal point around which all family processes revolved. He described how these beliefs and roles went unchallenged by family members in spite of reality distortions required to keep the myth intact. Myths were thought to offer a rationale for familial behavior while concealing their true motives, i.e., their homeostatic and defensive functions (1966). Family myths were also seen as providing ritual formulas for action at certain crisis points in the family's development.

Although Ferreira was the first to link the concept of myth to family processes, fascination with the psychology of myth among individually oriented therapists has been longstanding. The centrality of the Oedipus myth in Freud's psychoanalytic formulations is well known. Myths and symbols have consistently been used to understand the individual's attempts to deal with unconscious, intrapsychic conflicts (Fenichel, 1945; Freud, 1924; Jung, 1968; Klein, 1975). Personal myths have been viewed as developing

Stephen A. Anderson, PhD, is Director of the Marital and Family Therapy Training Program and Associate Professor at the University of Connecticut, School of Family Studies, U-117, 843 Bolton Road, Storrs, CT 06268. Dennis A. Bagarozzi, PhD, is in private practice at the Alliance for Counseling and Therapeutic Services (ACTS), 42 Lenox Pointe, Atlanta, GA 30324.

3

around unresolved developmental crises (Anderson & Bagarozzi, 1983; Bagarozzi & Anderson, 1982; Bettelheim, 1975; Jung 1968; Jung & Kerenyi, 1949; Neumann, 1954a, 1954b) and Bettelheim (1975) has proposed that the symbols found in the language of myths appeal simultaneously to our conscious and unconscious minds.

Many have viewed myth not only as a link to the deeper levels of unconscious, but to the secrets and mysteries of life itself. For instance, Jung (1968) saw myth as a fundamental expression of a collective human nature and as a key to understanding it. Fromm (1951) has noted that an understanding of the symbolic language of myths brings us in touch with one of our most significant sources of wisdom and reveals to us the deeper layers of our own personalities. Others have drawn parallels between the motifs found in classical mythology and those which have characterized the struggle for personal identity over the course of history. The search for one's true self, for justice, and such themes as primordial oneness, cosmic conflict, heroic recovery from death, restoration of harmony, renewal and rebirth have been viewed as the very process of life and the gateway to its meaning (Ahsen, 1984; Campbell, 1949; Perry, 1976).

Definitions of personal myths have emphasized all of these various elements. Watts (1954) offers a definition of myth as a complex of stories, some no doubt fact and others fantasy, which human beings regard as demonstrations of the inner meaning of the universe and of human existence. Feinstein (1979) has defined personal myths as those cognitive structures that serve the functions of explaining, sacralizing and guiding the individual in a manner analogous to the role played by cultural myths in society. They give meaning to the past, define the present and provide direction for the future (Feinstein, 1979). Previously, we have described personal myths as symbolic reconstructions of one's past experiences (biological, familial, social and cultural) in a way which gives them some psychological order and meaning for that individual (Bagarozzi & Anderson, 1982). Central attributes of personal myths which suggest their widespread appeal among clinicians are: (1)

their emphasis on forward movement, development and self actualization and (2) their suggestion of magical solutions through their inherent richness of hidden, symbolic content and meaning (Ahsen, 1984).

Since Ferreira's original formulations, fascination with the concept of family myth among family therapists has remained. However, his original conceptual formulations have undergone considerable revision and expansion. For instance, Ferreira's (1963, 1966) formulations have been extended beyond their emphasis on defensive functions to include their morphogenetic potentials (Anderson & Bagarozzi, 1983; Bagarozzi & Anderson, 1982). The essential elements of myth such as symbol, metaphor, analogy and ritual have been examined in depth (Anderson & Bagarozzi, 1983; Angelo, 1981; Andolfi et al., 1983; van der Hart, 1978) and therapeutic interventions based upon the understanding of these various elements have been introduced (cf. Angelo, 1981; Keim et al., 1987; Kobak & Waters, 1984; Levick et al., 1981; O'Connor, 1984; O'Connor & Hoorwitz, 1984; Selvini-Palazzoli et al., 1977; 1978). Preliminary efforts also have been made to address the interrelationships among personal myths, conjugal myths and family system myths (Bagarozzi & Anderson, 1982).

The study of family myths draws its strength from a variety of theoretical and clinical orientations including anthropology (Seltzer & Seltzer, 1983; van der Hart, 1987), object relations theory (Boszormenyi-Nagy & Spark, 1973; Byng-Hall, 1973; Stierlin, 1973), and cognitive psychology (Feinstein, 1979). Family myths are frequently alluded to in systems conceptualizations of family behavior although they have not yet been afforded a central role in these formulations (cf. Boszormenyi-Nagy & Krasner, 1986; Hoffman, 1985; Kramer, 1985; Steinglass, 1978). Constructs related to family myths such as "ecology of ideas" (Bogden, 1984), paradigm (Reiss, 1981), frames (Coyne, 1985; Jones, 1986) or world views (Sluzki, 1983; Watzlawick, 1978) also have emerged. However, their links to the myth concept remain unexplored. Finally, empirical investigations concerning family myths are beginning to emerge. Several of the papers in this collection demonstrate initial attempts to research some aspects of this complex phenomenon.

It is our hope that this collection will sensitize clinicians to the important role the study of mythological systems can play in the future development of the family therapy field. There are a number of contemporary issues which can be addressed from a mythological perspective. First, the field has begun to re-emphasize the role of the individual in the family in contrast to an almost exclusive emphasis on the couple or family system (cf. Feldman, 1985; Massey, 1986; Pinsof & Catherall, 1986; Weeks, 1986). These authors and others consistently note the need to integrate individually oriented and interpersonally oriented concepts and techniques. Second, efforts have been made to integrate the various "schools" of family therapy (Breunlin & Schwartz, 1986; Frazer, 1982; Stanton, 1981). Third, the emphasis in the field is shifting from an exclusive attention to interactional pattern to an appreciation for the parallel role played by patterned perceptual processes (the creation of meaning, paradigms, world views, frames etc.) (cf. Bogden, 1984; Cade, 1986; Jones, 1986; Watzlawick, 1984). As Hoffman (1985) notes, "mental phenomena have been brought back from a long exile, and ideas, beliefs, attitudes, feelings, premises, values, and myths have been declared central again" (p. 390).

The authors of papers presented in this collection offer a variety of formulations regarding both personal and family myths in an attempt to bridge the chasms between individual, couple and family systems dynamics. Similarly, the therapeutic methods derived from this way of conceptualizing family process are not school specific (i.e., are not restricted to a single school of therapy). All these authors seem to share the belief that a heightened appreciation for the family's symbolic system of meaning broadens the therapist's point of view and expands his or her options for understanding and treating individuals', couples' and families' presenting problems. These views do not preclude the therapist choosing to attend primarily to a specific aspect of interpersonal dynamics such as the redundant patterns of interaction within the system which maintain symptomatic behaviors (strategic models) or to incongruities in the family's hierarchy or organizational structure (structural models). While not disregarding the directional influence such behavioral changes can have on cognitive schema (Beck et al., 1979; Ellis & Grieger, 1977; Meichenbaum, 1977), this view also emphasizes the power of attending to cognitive structures and perceptual experience as a central ingredient to lasting behavior change (Beck et al., 1979; Ellis & Grieger, 1977; Meichenbaum, 1977).

Focus on the myth aspect of systems functioning should not take attention away from the conscious, shared belief systems of family members or the internal dialogues of individuals. These conscious processes are seen as including important elements of myths that shape current behaviors. It is possible for therapists to work with some individuals or families at conscious, cognitive levels of awareness through education, reframing, interpretation or experiential exercises, and still help them become more aware of the role mythologies play in shaping their life courses. Such conscious recognition of operative myths, in some cases, may be enough to facilitate modification, or the accommodation of existing myth structures to new information and environmental input. Alternatively, the conscious highlighting of dissonant or conflicting mythical themes may, following a period of disequilibrium, lead to the incorporation of previously existing elements into a new, more functional mythological structure with greater cognitive complexity.

The view of mythological systems proposed in most of these papers also emphasizes the "unconscious," or out of awareness, components of families' shared experiences. Clinical attention to these alternative levels of experience, through analogical and symbolic forms of communication, can play a direct role in modifying family members' behaviors while bypassing the logical, conscious, left-hemispheric aspects of the cognitive system. For example, the use of symbolically meaningful ritual prescriptions, rites of passage, paradoxical interventions or the elaboration and exaggeration of metaphors and symbols are powerful vehicles for editing mythological themes and inducing behavioral change (Anderson & Russell, 1982; Anderson & Bagarozzi, 1983; Bagarozzi & Anderson, 1982).

We strongly believe that marital and family therapists must begin to attend to the symbolic and affective components of human relationships as a way to introduce potential change. Intervention strategies that push families toward an intensification of their cognitive and emotional experiences are critical for inducing creative, second-order leaps to new or revised personal and family mythologies. Kobak and Waters (1984) have associated the process of maintaining the intensity in therapy with the "liminal" stage in ritual development where much that is bound by habitual processes is liberated. Through the use of evocatory instruments and notable personalities (relics, momentos, heroes, ancestors, fairy tales, favorite books or movies) or the exaggeration of typical behaviors, memories or symbols far beyond the family's previous understandings, the therapist is able to maintain an element of "mystery" (Kobak & Waters, 1984), "magic" (Seltzer & Seltzer, 1983), unpredictability and an element of danger (O'Connor & Hoorwitz, 1984) which can create profound shifts in families' perceptions of the world and consequently their behavior. Preliminary empirical evidence has pointed to the importance of intervention strategies which maintain a degree of intensity at a level greater than the family's usual tolerance level as a critical factor in producing positive therapeutic outcomes (Anderson et al., 1985). The methods used to maintain this level of intensity and to effect families' mythological systems are explored in detail here.

Readers intrigued by the papers presented here will find that they are not faced with a task of learning "new techniques" or another model of therapy. The critical task of one interested in the mythological approach discussed here is to draw upon his or her understanding of the nonobjective, symbolic, analogical, creative, right hemispheric and unconscious elements of experience. Unconscious does not refer here to repressed or denied aspects of experience but to the Jungian, Ericksonian emphasis on the creative life force inherent in all living things. Such an approach requires attention to the multiple levels of meaning inherent in each statement, behavior or gesture and a willingness to play with words, objects or dearly held values or points of view.

The authors chosen for inclusion in this collection of papers are those who have focused specifically on myths as the focal point around which their work revolves. While other authors (particularly those who emphasize an intergenerational perspective in their work) have dealt with the concept of myth, their emphasis tends to focus on marital or family interactional patterns. Unfortunately, the role of symbolic systems of meaning has not been clearly distinguished from these transgenerational behavioral patterns. Therefore, the methods of clinical intervention developed by these schools of therapy have tended to overlook the importance of symbolism in the formulation of treatment strategies.

The papers presented here can be thought of as comprising two general categories: (1) conceptual formulations and clinical application, and (2) empirical studies.

In the first selection, Wencke Seltzer, a noted Norwegian therapist, presents her most recent formulation regarding a specific class of mythical themes: "Myths of Destruction: A Cultural Approach to Families in Therapy." She underlines the universality of such myths for whole cultures and links the archetypical themes of destruction to a cleansing process which is followed by a fresh beginning, free from earlier contamination. Such themes, at the macro level, are assumed to manifest at the individual and family level as latent, unconscious prescriptions which perpetuate the past; constrain family members' ways of thinking, feeling and behaving; and yet offer clues to unnegotiated family transitions and adaptations. Her cultural approach to therapy seeks to restore fluidity to family systems by restoring the family's ability to operate at both the material (ritualized, interactional) and ideational (belief and perceptual) levels of family life. She postulates that by attending to the implicit, subvocal, mythical themes that "code" family members' behaviors, therapists are able to "unfreeze" the family's stasis. This allows new information to be processed by the family system. Making the implicit explicit, using metaphorical and symbolic language, and creating evocatory images all facilitate therapeutic intervention at the ideational level.

Seltzer presents a case where an acting out youngster is described as possessing a "golden egg" inside himself. This "golden egg" metaphor is symbolically and emotionally charged and carries with it an implicit message that within the boy there exists a "jewel." This "jewel" is as much a part of his permanent character as his character disorder and has the potential for "new life" if it is just nurtured and allowed to hatch.

The second paper by Andlofi and Angelo entitled, "Family Myth, Metaphor and the Metaphoric Object in Therapy," portrays myths as a complex of real events, historical recollections, and imagined roles and characteristics which condense around unresolved problems of loss, separation, abandonment, individuation, nourishment and deprivation. These Italian authors view myth as a model of values and prescriptive functions, a "code," an internal "narrative" or "matrix of consciousness" that organizes interpretations of "reality." The essential building blocks of these mythological codes are symbols and metaphors. The authors describe the use of metaphoric objects in therapy as a pretext for entering into shared myths and for transmitting a series of messages that transcend the literal contents of a family's narrative and bring to light missing elements of the essential plot. The choice of a metaphoric object is a creative act by which the therapist introduces potentially new or previously fragmented information which in turn can lead to a new or revised code for interpreting the reality experienced among family members. A case is presented where a chair was used as a "throne" to graphically portray the dysfunctional hierarchical structure of the family, to highlight the replication of unresolved issues from previous generations, and to accentuate the parts played by each member in the family drama until they become charged with meaningful emotion. These interventions enabled the family to make a much needed hierarchical reorganization.

The third paper by van der Hart, Witztum and de Voogt entitled, "Myths and Rituals: Anthropological Views and Their Application in Strategic Family Therapy," uses the notion of myths being traditional oral tales told by family members about the family and its members. Rituals are defined as prescribed symbolic acts that must be performed in a certain way and in a certain sequence in order for family stability to be maintained. These rituals may or may not be accompanied by verbal formulas. Based upon a review of the anthropological literature, these authors emphasize the ceremonial and symbolic nature of myth and ritual. Rituals, because of their connections to both the material (interactional) plane of family culture and to the ideational (symbolic) level of family culture, are viewed as offering a direct method for altering both the family's behaviors and shared constructs of reality.

Therapy itself is viewed as a ritual healing process which includes the family's mythical story about the presenting problem and how it came about, the ritual actions by the healer (therapist), other members of the community (e.g., family members) and the patient which enact transformations in the patient's inner experience and the social relationships in which he is an integral part. Ritualized actions by the therapist which are used to bring about desired changes include (a) an elaboration of the existing family myth, (b) the presentation of a modified therapeutic version of the myth which serves as a substitute for the family's existing dysfunctional myth, and (c) the prescription of a therapeutic ritual which complements the symbolic elements of the therapeutic myth and enacts its material (interactional) elements.

Van der Hart, Witztum and de Voogt present a case study where a therapeutic myth is prescribed without the accompanying therapeutic ritual. Though a positive outcome was achieved, the authors argue that the results could have been enhanced had intervention also included some type of symbolic ritual.

In "Mythmaking in the Land of Imperfect Specialness: Lions, Laundry Baskets and Cognitive Deficits," Janine Roberts illustrates how families evidence a variety of interrelated myths and daily rituals. In her in-depth case study, she illustrates how a number of intervention strategies such as therapeutic rituals, story retelling, fables, puppet shows, symbol elaboration, and problem-solving training can be used to edit family myths. Her extensive follow-up of the family, several years after termination, provides an uncommon opportunity to examine clients' retrospective accounts of the benefits derived from a mythological approach to therapy.

The paper by Feinstein and Krippner entitled "Personal Myths— In the Family Way," offers a structured approach to working with individuals and families in therapy or in workshop settings. Their conceptualization of personal mythologies as cognitive structures that explain the world, guide personal development and establish a relationship with the mysteries of existence, allow these authors to integrate recent trends in cognitive psychology with the mythic motifs that have evolved over the history of our culture and of human consciousness. They offer a number of innovative approaches to working with clients' personal mythologies. These include guided imagery, symbolic ceremonies, daily rituals, fairy tale and dream analysis, role playing, behavioral rehearsals and behavioral contracting. In their final discussion, they examine the underlying forces in contemporary society that are of particular significance to the mythic life of individuals, families and clinicians and how these may become both catalysts for, or inhibitors of social change.

The first empirically based presentation in this collection entitled, "Reality and Myth in Family Life: Changes Across Generations," is by Frederick Wamboldt and Steven Wolin. These authors see family myths as recollections, perceptions and interpersonal tendencies that individuals internalize in childhood and retain throughout their lives. They reserve the term "family reality" for the family group level of analysis. Based on research conducted by their colleagues at George Washington University over the last twenty years, Wamboldt and Wolin view the family's reality as an objective, group-level construction that organizes a family's experience and coordinates its actions. They note that the family reality cannot be discussed in words, but must be inferred from observations of the family's behavior. Family myths are considered a characteristic of individuals' own unique stories of their families.

The authors present a theory of mate selection and premarital behavior based upon the partners' family myths. Each person enters the relationship with a particular posture. These postures (e.g., accept and continue, process and struggle or disengage from and repudiate) must be integrated through a transactional process, to form a new conjugal/family reality. Preliminary data from their research project on mate selection and early marriage is discussed along with hypotheses regarding the prognosis for couples who assume each of the different postures.

The final paper by Bagarozzi and Anderson, is entitled "Personal, Conjugal and Family Myths: Theoretical, Empirical and Clinical Developments." In this paper, the authors present their theoretical formulations regarding the development, maintenance and evolution of personal, conjugal and family myths. Personal myths are defined as complexes of symbolic and affectively-laden themes regarding the *self*, the *self-in-relation to significant others* and the self's *internalized ideals of significant others*. The coming together of themes from two personal mythologies becomes the foundation for the development of a unique conjugal mythology. One's cognitive representations of the *ideal spouse* and the *ideal marriage* are viewed as playing a central role in the development of a couple's conjugal mythology. Family myths are thought to emerge from the meshing and integration of all family members' personal myths, the conjugal myths of the parents and the shared experiences of all family members as a group. Here, the parents' idealized expectations for each child play a pivotal role.

This paper is also intended to introduce readers to the empirical research, assessment procedures and some of the intervention strategies the authors have developed after a decade of working from a mythological perspective.

At the end of the collection, we have added a resource section. First, Gary Steck reviews earlier, original papers on family myths. Then, Stephen Gavazzi outlines seminal articles from the intergenerational family therapy perspective. Included are both original theoretical papers which have influenced the evolution of the family myth concept and recent empirical work which has begun to test some of the intergenerational model's central hypotheses.

REFERENCES

Ahsen, A. (1984). *Trojan Horse: Imagery in psychology, art, literature and politics*. New York: Brandon House.

Anderson, S.A. & Russell, C.S. (1982). Utilizing process and content in designing paradoxical interventions. *American Journal of Family Therapy, 10*, 48-60.

Anderson, S.A. & Bagarozzi, D.A. (1983). The use of family myths as an aid to strategic therapy. *Journal of Family Therapy, 5*, 145-154.

Anderson, S.A., Atilano, R.B., Paff-Bergen, L., Russell, C.S. & Jurich, A.P. (1985). Dropping out of marriage and family therapy: Intervention strategies and spouses' perceptions. *American Journal of Family Therapy, 13*, 39-54.

Andolfi, M., Angelo, C., Menghi, P. & Nicolo-Corigliano, A.M. (1983). *Behind the family mask*. New York: Brunner/Mazel.

Angelo, C. (1981). The use of the metaphoric object in family therapy. *American Journal of Family Therapy, 9*, 69-78.

Bagarozzi, D.A. & Anderson, S.A. (1982). The evolution of family mythological systems: Considerations for meaning, clinical assessment and treatment. *Journal of Psychoanalytic Anthropology, 5*, 71-90.

Beck, A.T., Rush, A.J., Shaw, B.F. & Emery, G. (1979). *Cognitive therapy of depression*. New York: Guilford Press.

Bettleheim, B. (1975). *The uses of enchantment: The meaning and importance of fairy tales*. New York: Knoph.

Bogdan, J.L. (1984). Family organization as an ecology of ideas: An alternative of the reification of family systems. *Family Process, 23*, 375-388.

Boszormenyi-Nagy, I. & Krasner, B.R. (1986). *Between give and take: A clinical guide to contextual therapy*. New York: Brunner/Mazel.

Breunlin, D.C. & Schwartz, R.C. (1986). Sequences: Toward a common denominator of family therapy. *Family Process, 25*, 67-87.

Byng-Hall, J. (1973). Family myths used as defense in conjoint family therapy. *British Journal of Medical Psychology, 46*, 239-250.

Cade, B. (1986). The reality of "reality" (or the "reality" of reality). *American Journal of Family Therapy, 14*, 49-56.

Campbell, J. (1949). *The hero with a thousand faces*. New York: Pantheon Books.

Coyne, J.C. (1985). Toward a theory of frames and reframing: The social nature of frames. *Journal of Marital and Family Therapy, 11*, 337-344.

Ellis, A. & Grieger, R. (1977). *RET: Handbook of rational emotive therapy*. New York: Springer.

Feinstein, A.D. (1979). Personal mythology as a paradigm for a holistic public psychology. *American Journal of Orthopsychiatry, 49*, 198-217.

Feldman, L.B. (1985). Integrative multi-level therapy: A comprehensive interpersonal and intrapsychic approach. *Journal of Marital and Family Therapy, 11*, 357-372.

Fenichel, O. (1945). *The psychoanalytic theory of neurosis*. New York: W. W. Norton.

Ferreira, A.J. (1963). Family myth and homeostasis. *Archives of General Psychiatry, 9*, 457-463.

Ferreira, A.J. (1966). Family myths. *Psychiatric Research Report of the American Psychiatric Association, 20*, 85-90.

Fraser, J. (1982). Structural and strategic family therapy: A basis for marriage or grounds for divorce. *Journal of Marital and Family Therapy, 8*, 13-22.

Freud, S. (1924). *Collected papers*. London: Institute of Psychoanalysis and Hogarth Press.

Fromm, E. (1951). *The forgotten language: An introduction to the understanding of dreams, fairy tales and myths*. New York: Grove Press.

Hoffman, L. (1985). Beyond power and control: Toward a "second order" family systems therapy. *Family Systems Medicine, 3*, 381-396.

Jones, C.W. (1986). Frame cultivation: Helping new meanings take root in families. *American Journal of Family Therapy, 14*, 57-68.

Jung, C. (1968). The archetypes and the collective unconscious (*Collected Works, Vol. 9, part 1, 2nd ed.*; R. Hull, trans.).

Jung, C. & Kerenyi, C. (1949). *Essays on a science of mythology*. New York: Pantheon Books.

Keim, I., Lentine, G., Keim, J. & Madanes, C. (1987). Strategies for changing the past. *Journal of Strategic and Systemic Therapies, 6*, 2-17.

Klein, M. (1975). *Love, guilt and reparation & other works 1921-1945.* London: Hogarth Press and the Institute of Psycho-Analysis.

Kobak, R.R. & Waters, D.B. (1984). Family therapy as a rite of passage: Play's the thing. *Family Process, 23*, 89-100.

Kramer, J.R. (1985). *Family interfaces: Transgenerational patterns.* New York: Brunner/Mazel.

Levick, S.E., Jalali, B. & Strauss, J.S. (1981). With onions and tears: A multidimensional analysis of a counter-ritual. *Family Process, 20*, 77-83.

Massey, R.F. (1986). What/who is the family system? *American Journal of Family Therapy, 14*, 23-39.

Meichenbaum, D. (1977). *Cognitive-behavior modification: An integrated approach.* New York: Plenum Press.

Neumann, E. (1954a). *The origins and history of consciousness*, Vol. I. New York: Harper & Row.

Neumann, E. (1954b). *The origins and history of consciousness: The psychological stages and the evolution of consciousness*, Vol. II. New York: Harper & Row.

O'Connor, J.J. (1984). The resurrection of a magical reality: Treatment of functional migraine in a child. *Family Process, 23*, 501-509.

O'Connor, J.J. & Hoorwitz, A.N. (1984). The bogeyman cometh: A strategic approach for difficult adolescents. *Family Process, 23*, 237-249.

Perry, J.W. (1976). *Roots of renewal in myth and madness.* San Francisco: Jossey-Bass.

Pinsof, W.M. & Catherall, D.R. (1986). The Integrative psychotherapy alliance: Family, couple and individual therapy scales. *Journal of Marital and Family Therapy, 12*, 137-151.

Reiss, D. (1981). *The family's construction of reality.* Cambridge, MA: Harvard University Press.

Seltzer, W.J. & Seltzer, M.R. (1983). Magic, material, and myth. *Family Process, 22*, 3-14.

Seltzer, W.J. (1985). Conversion disorder in childhood and adolescence: A familial/cultural approach Part 1. *Family Systems Medicine, 3*, 261-280.

Selvini Palazzoli, M., Boscolo, L., Cecchin, G. & Prata, G. (1977). Family rituals: A powerful tool in family therapy. *Family Process, 16*, 445-453.

Selvini Palazzoli, M., Boscolo, L., Cecchin, G. & Prata, G. (1978). A ritualized prescription in family therapy: Odd days and even days. *Journal of Marriage and Family Counseling, 4*, 3-9.

Sluzki, C. (1983). Process, structure and world views: Toward an integrated view of systemic models in family therapy. *Family Process, 22*, 469-476.

Stanton, M.D. (1981). An integrated structural/strategic approach to family therapy. *Journal of Marital and Family Therapy, 7*, 427-439.

Steinglass, P. (1978). The conceptualization of marriage from a systems theory perspective. In T.J. Paolino & B.S. McCrady (Eds.), *Marriage and marital therapy*. New York: Brunner/Mazel.

Stierlin, H. (1973). Group fantasies and family myths: Some theoretical and practical aspects. *Family Process, 12*, 111-125.

van der Hart, O. (1978). *Rituals in psychotherapy: Transition and continuity*. New York: Irvington.

van der Hart, O. (1987). *Coping with loss; The therapeutic use of leavetaking rituals*. New York: Irvington.

Watts, A. (1954). *Myth and ritual in Christianity*. New York: MacMillan.

Watzlawick, P. (1978). *The language of change*. New York: Basic Books.

Watzlawick, P. (1984). *The invented reality*. New York: W.W. Norton.

Weeks, G.R. (1986). Individual-system dialectic. *American Journal of Family Therapy, 14*, 5-12.

Myths of Destruction:
A Cultural Approach
to Families in Therapy

Wencke J. Seltzer

SUMMARY. This paper describes a recent formulation regarding a specific class of mythical themes, myths of destruction. A case study is presented to illustrate how a cultural approach to therapy can be used to edit the destructive myth and "unfreeze" the family's stasis.

THE BOY WITH THE GOLDEN EGG INSIDE

A boy of fourteen years was brought into a child and adolescent clinic in the municipal health system of Oslo, Norway, accompanied by his mother and stepfather. The family wanted help with the boy who had been involved in theft, sniffing and the use of hard drugs. The boy had been truant from school for a long period of time, and presently, his school attendance had ceased completely. After many attempts at helping the boy, the parents had now come to the conclusion that the boy needed to be placed in an institution where his destructive behavior could be controlled. They did not feel they could handle him at home any longer. The therapist who had been working with the family for some time, felt that he had gotten into a repetitive cycle where good suggestions were ac-

Wencke J. Seltzer is Chief Psychologist, Oslo Helserad, Central Division for Child and Adolescent Psychiatry, Trondhjemsveien 2, Oslo, Norway.

The case reported on in this article was treated at the Stovner Polyclinic for Child and Adolescent Psychiatry, Oslo Helserad, Oslo, Norway. Many thanks are directed to the main therapist in the case, Arne Hoyland, Chief Psychologist, and the team of colleagues of that clinic.

17

cepted by the family, but had no effect. The pattern of the boy's destructive behavior repeated itself, and despite good intentions, it seemed that this pattern could not be altered.

In an attempt to become free of this vicious cycle, the therapist called upon a team of colleagues and a supervisor, to look in on a session from behind the oneway screen. The task of the team was to observe as "fresh outsiders," bringing new ideas into the situation. Since this was a therapeutic process which, at this stage, had become frozen into stasis, the team felt it was important for the current perspective of the situation to be altered.

The team served much like a group of anthropologists doing field work. As in any other anthropological inquiry, the culture of study served as its own informant (Seltzer & Seltzer, 1983). The family in this case, and to some degree the therapist, were considered informants of familial lifeways; patterns of feeling, believing and acting. The therapist, as an established workmate to the family, and someone familiar with their "established" familial patterns, had long ago passed the border of someone in the role of "naive" newcomer to the family. If the therapist had started to "backtrack" in order to develop new ways of understanding, the family most likely would have perceived this as a betrayal of the working relationship developed in the therapeutic system of family and therapist. In a sense, the therapist had become a part of the established familial culture.

However, the license to ask "naive" questions was issued to the team of colleagues by the therapist and the family. The agreement was that the team would be free to ask questions and/or pursue issues which it sensed were important. The supervisor would be the one to enter the session and communicate the voice of the team to the therapeutic system. The therapist would continue to sit with the family, more as part of their system than as a part of the colleague system. The therapist was therefore not responsible for the points made by the team. Yet, he served as a safe "bridge" between the established and the new in this potential stage of transition. The family was frozen into a rigid pattern of behavior and needed to be revitalized into new lifeways. The addition of the team into the session obviously left them vulnerable and at risk of change. Change here would imply a period of marginality, where nothing safe would be left to hold on to. It was in this context that the somewhat more moderate and conservative position held by the therapist served as a stabilizing factor, allowing the family to be more available for the risky endeavor of opening up for novel exploration into their family fortress.

The team's task was to watch carefully all nonverbal behavior, listen carefully to the language of the family, and be keenly aware of implicit meaning embedded in the verbally expressed information offered by the familial culture and the therapist. Further, the team was, at this point, not focusing on practical solutions to the problem as defined by the family. The team was more interested in expressing their own free associations as they came up during the session. These associations were based on observations made of the therapeutic system and also on impressions loosely formed from the material offered by the family. The supervisor served as a gatherer of all these responses and had as her task, to put the bits and pieces together into possible themes.

The main observation made by the team rather early in the session was a strong impression that the boy did not fit the description of a hardened criminal youth. Furthermore, the parents who said they wanted their boy removed from the family, communicated a great deal of warmth and caring for the boy, seemingly drawing the boy into the family rather than expelling him. There seemed to be a discrepancy between what the family explicitly said, and their actual behavior. The team felt strongly that this was not a situation where the parents were truly ready to expel their young son from the family. It was as if the parents were directed by a predetermined "code," carefully hidden in a family ideology where the youth "naturally" had to behave in such a way that an institution would have to take care of him. The affect of the session was very sad, as if the family was faced with an unavoidable social funeral. With this as a point of departure, the team proceeded to "push" the family's ideational system in the hope that a better understanding of this unknown "code" could be revealed and therapeutically manipulated.

The supervisor entered the therapy session, maintaining her position as a curious outsider who wanted to know more about the family lifeways. In order not to deviate too much from the pattern already exhibited by the family, the supervisor turned to the boy, and talked to the family/therapeutic system through him. She said the team behind the screen felt that he followed a kind of preset program for his antisocial activities. She wanted to know in detail what the plan of the program was, how it was going to be carried out, and how much time he was giving himself before the plan would be fulfilled.

After a somewhat laborious verbalization of a "program" uttered by the boy, the parents broke in to help. This led to their volunteering a part of the family history which seemed extremely painful for them to expose. It turned out that the mother had two older sons with criminal careers. Both were in prison at this time. This story was further linked with the biological father who had disappeared from the family when the boys were still preschoolers. This father was described as irresponsible, possessing a devious character, and someone that no one should have to inherit in terms of genetic material. During the boys' growing years, the mother had felt very much alone and overwhelmed with the task of raising three sons in a complex modern society. She expressed a true sense of failure and resignation regarding the future of her boys. The implicit message was, that this time, it was better to facilitate the placement of the youngest son, before the family again had to be imposed upon by authorities to deal with criminal behavior. Then the family would be dissolved and the predetermined "doom of destruction" would be fulfilled.

The stepfather was visibly touched by the implications of this story. It turned out that the stepfather had never been given a family mandate to intervene in the daily tasks of raising the boy, despite the fact that he had been living in the family for the past several years. At the same time, it was clear through the observations made by the team, that the stepfather was emotionally involved with the boy in a positive way, and that he was a person the boy tended to turn to.

To the question raised by the supervisor as to who was the boy's father, the boy, with tears in his eyes, answered that he never had a father. This led to a discussion in the session between the therapist and the supervisor about what it meant to be a father in some families, and what it might mean in this particular family. Through the team behind the screen, it was suggested that in this day and age, many youths had fathers who were not biologically related, but who still functioned as good parents.

In this family's ideational sphere, the concept of father was a touchy one, not available for open discussion. "Father" was linked rigidly with biology and synonymous with "defective character." Furthermore, the disappearance of the father seemed to be linked with sadness and unfinished grief for the boys, a topic which appeared to be taboo in this family. The idea that the father had left in the boys a preset defective character which could not be escaped, resulted in the boy crying openly and the parents speaking in a soft tone of voice. This was in contrast to their previously forceful voices.

The therapist and the supervisor then continued their wondering about the "preset program" the family seemed directed by, and asked again how much time the boy had to finish the plan. The boy continued crying and said he missed his middle brother. This brother was "taken by authorities and put in prison" when he was a few months older than the primary patient's current age. The therapist and supervisor then noted that the boy did not have much time left to complete his task and thereby remain loyal to the implicit beliefs of the family.

The boy had apparently taken it upon himself to expose this implicit side of the family ideology to the external world. This led to a period of silence in the session, accompanied by tears. The therapist and supervisor again discussed this issue and said that they thought the boy's brothers were possibly also directed by a preset program which, at an earlier time, was unavoidable. However, perhaps things could be different in the family today. It could be that the family was now at a stage where the course of events could take a different turn. Beside the fact that the family now had a father, the supervisor said that she felt the fourteen-year-old boy "had a golden egg inside." This egg was ready to shine and be shown to the world with all its good qualities. It could shine best with the light thrown upon it within the present family. However, the question was whether the family was ready to provide the nest for such a gift. The supervisor then said she would have to return to her place behind the looking glass. Sometimes things had to be seen from a distance, in order for hidden jewels to be detected.

During the following sessions, the question of placing the boy out of the family was no longer a part of the familial "plan of action." On the contrary, the family reported a great deal of optimism for their present family as an intact unit. The boy had not engaged in any of his previously antisocial activities. The boy and his stepfather had spent much time together. In addition, the family and the therapist had met with the school and a program had been carefully tailored to the boy's capacities at this stage of his development. At the time of this writing, more than a year later, the boy was still living at home with his parents, continuing to do well in school, and had not engaged in antisocial behavior.

MYTHS OF DESTRUCTION

Myths predicting the end of man, like myths explaining the origin of man, appear to be universal. Religious themes and other institutionalized belief systems commonly adhered to in various cultures, often include the idea that a final day of judgement will appear. In Norse mythology, Snorres (1973) described Ragarokk. Ragarokk was the final battle between man and the gods on one side, and the evil creatures named "Jotner" on the other side which ended with the destruction of man and his gods. In modern society, the idea of doomsday is still alive. Many religious sects preach as their most central theme, the final day of judgement as an unavoidable event in the future. Paradoxically, themes of destruction inherently indicate that following the end, a new beginning appears. Destruction appears to contain a cleansing process followed by a fresh beginning, free of contamination. Thus, the end as well as the beginning may be understood as mutually dependent marking points, patterned in a circular process, where one is inconceivable without the other.

At this macro-level of institutionalized belief systems in cultures, myths are likely to be spelled out, accompanied by ritualistic ceremonies or expressed through other forms of symbolic manipulation. As an illustration, a man dressed in a particular robe is observed in a kneeling position, head bent down, and with folded hands. The cultural context of the event, the particulars of his costume, his statue-like bodily positioning, and his overall behavior signify to the observer a specific set of beliefs. The ritual is loaded with meaning, and so specifically communicated, that an observer familiar with the cultural context in which the event is taking place, will be able to infer rather accurately, themes of beliefs signified through the man's actions. Thus, in this instance, the man's beliefs become available for observation, not through a verbal account, but through a ritualistic account.

At a micro-level, in their meetings with individuals, small groups and families, practicing clinicians often encounter what this author has chosen to call myths of destruction. Contrary to more globally adhered to myths as described above, familial myths may not be available for observation in the sense that they are verbally recounted or expressed ritualistically in therapy sessions. Myths encountered by clinicians in small cultural units such as families entering therapy, are likely to take on a more private character, often existing at a subverbal level. Yet, these myths are powerful in their latent presence, buried in the collective unconscious of the familial culture. Myths as indicated by Freud (1955) as well as Levi-Strauss (1985), may be a kind of collective dream with hidden meaning. The hidden meaning may be inconsistent with conscious experience. Levi-Strauss (1966) suggests that familial cultures transmit myths subconsciously from the collective subconscious of the older generation to younger generations. In the experience of therapists, it is often these subconscious and hidden ideations which powerfully direct self-fulfilling prophesies in familial cultures.

Levi-Strauss applies the term "orchestra score" to designate a mythical corpus (1966, 1968). Elder bearers of a culture, through collective institutionalized practices, subconsciously transmit basic messages to the younger generation. The detailed content of the message, as interpreted by this author, is not of importance. This may not be known to the receiver of the message, but the total corpus of the ideation is transmitted and filled with the particular content relevant in the present context of the culture bearer.

Although this "score" may have originated in the past and may be tied to particular events of that history, it is the transmission of that basic "score" or "code," which may have the power of directing familial lifeways in the present. Thus, myth is "timeless" in terms of the power it has in influencing human cultures. Small children may act out or otherwise express mythical familial themes, without access to specific content or temporal history. Similarly, it is in this mythical scheme, as described by Henrik Ibsen (1881) that hidden ghosts from the past may turn up. Furthermore, myth may also be inconsistent with formal knowledge or that learned via science or other investigative attempts at reaching "truths." In this sense, myth may be irrational and operate according to its own logic. In therapeutic practice, this means that it is difficult if not futile, to explain away deeply rooted beliefs by reference to "modern scientific knowledge." This view of myth is contradictory to the popular view of myth as untruthful. Thus, it seems that myth may have implicit themes embedded within, that may be more fundamental in its relation to actual behaviors in familial cultures than those themes which are expressed in explicit opinions, beliefs or feelings and are accessible for discussion.

Again and again, therapists meet families where lifeways take turns which seem unavoidable and yet unexplainable. Thus, we see children develop curious symptoms of social or physical character. We see themes of previous generations repeated by a particular cultural code even though the concrete content may be altered, and the primary actors may be gone. As a clinician, this author could report on numerous cases where unconscious subverbal myths of destruction appear so powerful in directing familial lifeways that help from the outside is necessary in order to free the family from the grip of the invisible myth. In a study carried out by this author on fifteen families containing a child or adolescent with severe conversion disorder, myths of destruction appeared as common themes shared by these family cultures. The reader is referred to this study for further understanding of this author's conceptualization of the term familial culture as well as the application of the cultural approach in therapy (Seltzer, 1985a, 1985b).

Common to subverbal mythical themes is the capacity to freeze development of a familial group into stasis; narrow and locked ways of feeling, thinking and acting. Subverbal mythical themes may penetrate, dominate and direct total lifeways of family cultures, and block external and internal demands for adaptation. Myth, in this sense, is not only interesting in terms of its structural composition as it may be for sociologists and anthropologists. In the hands of a therapist, myth offers powerful tools for intervening therapeutically and transforming frozen familial cultures back into fluid ones.

LETHAL ELEMENTS IN HUMAN CULTURES

Lethal elements in human cultures are well known to anthropologists. The concept of familial culture as potentially lethal, was, to this author's knowledge, first developed by Jules Henry (1956, 1965) as he applied anthropological methods to studying families with psychotic child/adolescent members. Earlier, Henry (1941) had described belief elements in a South American tribal culture which had the power to destroy the whole culture. Similar phenomenon from modern cultures and times include the tragedy in Jamestown where strong religious beliefs caused the group to kill their babies. Similarly, among the Shakers in the eastern United States, bodily touch was prohibited due to beliefs about contamination and the culture is about to become extinct. In a small island fishing community on the west coast of Norway, an eight-year-old boy was reported drowned, as the children who witnessed this drama failed to seek help from their elders out of obedience to the strong rule that adults must not be disturbed while sleeping. This was in the context of a culture where sleep was badly needed between strenuous fishing shifts (Caspersen, 1987). The rule was perceived by the children to be so rigid and uncompromising that obedience to it outweighed the life of their playmate. The rule, and the ideational context in which it operated, had physically lethal consequences.

The same potential for pathology and lethal extermination may be seen in familial cultures. Pathology is used here in the sense that a culture is observed to be stuck, frozen and locked into self-perpetuated physical or social destruction. Lethal refers here to social and psychological death as well as physical. It may in fact be difficult to distinguish the two from one another. The term lethal is usually associated with physical death exclusively. But, for instance, a child's withdrawal from school, friends, age appropriate activities and formal learning will place the child at such a distance from others in society, that there is a question of such a child's ability to survive in a complex modern society. The individual child, however, will not be able to carry out a lethal "code" or program without the participation of her or his cultural context. Again, the child acts, or fails to act, according to the biocultural embeddedness of which she or he is a part. Thus, when clinicians are confronted with such a situation, it is important that they be able to look at the totality larger than that of the individual, and intervene as well, at the larger level of social inclusion.

In larger cultural systems, anthropologists have referred to stalemated cultural conditions as "cultural involution." Here again, when culture bearers have lost fluidity within their own system and become blocked from further adaptation, intervention from the outside is commonly initiated by leaders of revitalization movements or revolutionary reforms (Turnball, 1972; Wallace, 1966).

THE CULTURAL APPROACH

In the case description of the "boy with the golden egg inside," as well as in the discussion of myths of destruction, culture as a framing concept has been central. This has been employed by this author as a way to understand and act upon the process of therapy in familial groups. Although this approach has been described elsewhere (Seltzer, 1983, 1984, 1985a, 1985b, 1987), a concentrated summary of some principles of this model will be attempted here.

The Family as a Cultural Unit

First of all, the family is understood as a culture, bearing a composition of biosocial history, some of which is unique to that particular familial group, and some of which is shared "in common with" a given society and larger culture. Culture refers here to a system of learned and shared patterns of behavior, thinking and feeling among a designated group of bearers. Furthermore, such patterned lifeways include subconscious as well as conscious processes. Cultural bearers are, in a sense, imprinted upon by a massive inscription with some parts legible, and some parts only implicitly present. The popular assumption that culture is somewhat like a club in which one can choose membership, or choose to be for or against, is a serious misconception. On the contrary, culture, familial or societal, constitutes an embedded totality in which individuals participate from birth on. Within this embeddedness, bearers act and are acted upon. The term "bearer," borrowed from anthropology, seems particularly accurate in this context. Individuals are simply "culture bearers." This implies unavoidable social belongingness, which may be valued as positive or negative by those involved.

In the late sixties and early seventies, an antipsychiatric movement pointed to the negative "imprisonment" of the individual in the family. In accordance with this movement, psychiatric treatment often focused on the "rescue" and physical separation of the designated patient from the family. A child who exhibited psychiatric disorder, for instance, was often removed from her/his family, and placed in extrafamilial institutions for treatment. A "parentectomy" was performed. Such interventions however, were still more related to a biomedical model of thinking and practicing than to a recognition of humans as culture bearers, and as parts of an intimate sociocultural context including the family and broader culture as well. In the early seventies, when David Cooper (1970) published his book entitled *The Death of the Family*, a statement of the damaging effect of the family on individuals and society in general, the unavoidable belongingness to familial ties were nevertheless expressed in the dedication of the book, where he thanked his brother and his family for staying with him and supporting him during the time when he experienced personal crises, "just as a true family should." Thus, culture, familial and otherwise, is a totality within which all of us exist, including writers and therapists, a totality within which a neutral stand is difficult if not impossible to maintain.

The Dialectic Relation Between Ideational and Material Planes of Culture

The cultural approach entails a dialectic relationship between two elements of the cultural configuration. These two ingredients are referred to as existing at a material and ideational plane (Seltzer & Seltzer, 1983). At the material plane of family culture are found those behaviors which are made explicit by the family, thus subject to direct observation. These behaviors may be more or less established as habitual in the family, and involve recursive patterned interactions within the family. Such patterns are most clearly represented by family rituals; particular procedures for action and reaction adhered to — in varying degrees — by family members. The ideational plane of family culture is the locus of nonmaterialized, hence nonobservable beliefs and affects shared wholly or differentially by the members of the family. It is along this plane that cognitions and affects associated with family rituals are localized in such forms as myths and thematic beliefs. It is along this plane that secrets, pseudo secrets and other familial history are recorded in such forms as origin and inheritance myths as well as other recollections of the "real" or "imagined" past of the family and its ancestors. Further, it is along this plane that hidden injuries of the familial past are buried (Seltzer, 1985). It is along the ideational plane that subverbal ideations have power and potency in directing familial prophesies, thus promoting or inhibiting further adaptation.

In most of the world's ethnographically recorded cultures, there appears to be a fluid exchange between the ideational and material sphere of culture. Actions of culture bearers appear to relate flexibly to ideology, and this exchange is conducive to change. These systems, with few exceptions, appear to be responsive to the dialectic tension between mutually influencing idea and action. This dialectic tension appears to possess enough resilience and fluidity between the two planes, that culture bearers are allowed to change and adapt to environmental alterations. Thus, the flexible access to fluid exchange between these ideational and material aspects of culture appears to be a prerequisite for adaptation.

Familial Cultures Entering Therapy: A Freeze in Dialectic Exchange Between Material and Ideational Planes

In familial cultures entering therapy, adaptation to biocultural demands for change often appears stalemated. This in turn, may be related to life phases where transitions from one phase to another, in the particular history of the family, represents threat. At such times family cultures appear to lose flexibility and become rigid in maintenance of the established. Thus, the family is less capable of adaptation. It is perhaps at such times that familial cultures expose symptoms in one or several culture bearers. At these times, when families come for help, family systems most often appear lifeless, stagnant and rigid. Material and ideational planes of family culture have fallen into a state where previous resilience between the two is suspended.

In some families, the site of those locks seems located more at the ideational plane, while in other families the site seems located at the material plane. A locked position at the ideational plane, may involve deeply value laden myths, thematic beliefs and otherwise emotionally laden verbal and subverbal sentiments. These, like crystalline nuclei, may assume a radiating outward effect, locking the family members in fixed interrelational postures. In practice, a clinician may recognize this condition in families where for instance strong loyalties, strong verbal definitions of togetherness and sameness are believed to exist in the family, and where ideologies of mutual support and care reign uncritically. These ideations may be so demanding and idyllic that the distance between preaching and practice becomes overwhelming. Such a situation is conducive to stasis. In other families, the site of blockage seems more material than ideational. Here, self-perpetuated rituals seem to serve as blocking generators. Clinicians may recognize such a condition in families where the definition of the problem is narrow and fixed, and where attempts to "solve" the problem are equally fixed. Problem solution in such cases takes on a ritualistic quality, in the sense that the same procedures are attempted again and again, each time ending in failure. Attempts at solving the problem have then become a part of the problem, and serve to further maintain that which is perceived as a problem.

CLINICAL APPLICATION: CONCLUDING REFLECTIONS

In the previously presented case, the family containing the "Boy with the Golden Egg Inside," clinical intervention followed an understanding based on a cultural-dialectic "reading" of the family system. The family in this case seemed to be locked at the material plane of culture. The dialectic resilience between this plane of culture and its inverted ideational plane seemed suspended. The boy had become the repository and "actor-outer" of sacred, taboo and seemingly inaccessible myths and thematic beliefs in the family. These themes involved pseudosecretive and partially subverbal beliefs concerning the male offspring in the family. They were "believed" to have been born with a defective character genetically coded for a criminal career. The criminal character was directly linked with familial events in the past, with the biological father and the older brothers as primary actors. The youngest boy, who at this time came as the designated patient, was currently the locus of an unarticulated prophecy of destruction in the family. He, following in the footsteps of his brothers, was headed for prison. The boy engaged in ritualistic criminal behavior, obediently acting out the dialectically inverted ideational plane of familial culture. Furthermore, there seemed to exist in this family an unarticulated doom for the future; that the boy's course toward a permanently criminal and self-destructive career was unavoidable.

In therapy, an overlooked resource in the family was explored. The family, at this time, had a new father living with them, who seemed warmly engaged toward the boy, but who was not given a clear mandate by the mother to participate as a parental figure in raising the child. In retrospect, one may wonder if this reluctance on the part of the mother to let her new male partner take part in the family as a father, was a way to protect this male "outsider" from being contaminated by the biologically related lot of men in the family. Thus, the family was blocked from adapting to this potentially positive factor. Therapeutic interventions addressed themselves to these "readings" of the family situation.

First of all, the team of colleagues and the supervisor, attempted to make the inverted ideational plane of culture *explicit*. This was done by "pushing" the boy to describe the preset "program" by which the team felt he was directed. This "pushing" engaged the adult unit in trying to explain. The mother then offered the information about her two older sons who had criminal careers. This information presumably had been relayed in previous therapy sessions as well. However, the potency of this information lay in the context of the present situation. The information served as a linkage between seemingly mystical and unexplainable behavior of the boy, and pseudosecretive and partially taboo familial history. The term pseudosecretive as used here refers to events in the family well known by all members, yet not available for open discussion. The "new" information brought into the session by the mother, served as a linkage in moving the locked situation from its seemingly unexplainable and unavoidable status, to one which engaged the family in looking at the situation from another perspective, implicitly opening up for other ways of handling the problem as well.

A flow of emotions such as grief, guilt and mourning related to the "loss" of the brothers was "unleashed." The "pushing" of the mythical ideational elements of the boy's and family's behavior, flipped the coin of dialectics from the rigid ritualized material plane, to a position where previously inaccessible, ideationally based mythical material surfaced, with the effect that its power in maintaining the "stuck" behavior at the material plane was deflated.

Furthermore, the biological father of the boy represented another locus of unarticulated myth. This myth appeared to include beliefs that the father had transmitted criminal genes to his offspring, and that this had inescapable consequences for the behavior of the boy. The belief that only a biological father could help mother do the job of parenting, tied the situation into an even stronger bind. Here, therapeutic intervention addressed the issue of what makes a father a father. Again, attempts were made to "push" latent beliefs into explicit form. The distinction was made between biological father and social father. This distinction may have been important in that it placed the two fathers in two separate camps, where competition between the two was not an issue, neither was it possible to substitute one for the other. For the mother, the distinction may have helped to strengthen the current husband's position as a true partner, who could stand by her side as a parental figure to the boy, and yet, could never become his biological father. In this perspective the need to protect the husband from "contamination" by the other men in the family was no longer an issue. The currently present adult male in the family could now begin to *act* as a father in addition to *feeling* like a father toward the boy.

The therapy session became a locus in time where the stepfather publicly, in the presence of, and witnessed by the therapist and observational team, legitimately entered the family as an executor of an important parental task, without risking, in the minds of family members, fusion with the biological father. Again, a fluid and more flexible exchange between belief and action resulted, and premises for adaptation to the "new" situation which included a resourceful father were established. Furthermore, the distinction between past times, when the brothers grew up, and the situation in the family today, including the new father, also seemed to be of value. This helped to free the family from the grip of history. The power built into the "timelessness" of myth was deflated by this stand.

The most dominating and generally radiating myth in this family appeared to be one which had to do with "defective character." This, it was felt, had a serious locking effect in the family, keeping the boy and the family trapped in repetitive vicious circles. As a therapist, this author is respectfully attentive toward the power built into such a deeply rooted unarticulated myth in families. Thus, it was felt that a rational discussion with the family regarding this issue, would not be sufficient in undoing the power of this myth. On the contrary, if therapy had engaged the family in discussion purely at an intellectual level, the family would have been placed in a defensive position.

The supervisor therefore attempted to reach the family via *metaphor*. a language which was not subject to intellectual or rational discussion, and not clearly placed in the conscious or subconscious sphere of ideational process. Furthermore, it was important that the message relayed through the metaphor clearly strike in the central heart of the issue. Thus, she said it was felt that the boy had a golden egg inside, and that this was best provided for in the context of the present family. In a sense, the myth was made material by imaginative visualization. It was made concrete, yet remained highly *symbolic*. In recorded tales around the world, the egg appears as a symbol of new life (Cirlot, 1971). An egg is potentially in its germinal phase, developing, in mutual exchange with its surroundings, a new beginning. Furthermore, the egg was placed *inside* the boy, emphasizing the image that it was a permanent part of his person in the same way "character" is. No doubt was left in those present, that an image had entered the session, which in a direct way redefined the "core character" of the boy. It was important to add that such jewels were sometimes best detected by someone from the outside, who could look in on the situation from a distance. This freed the parents from the responsibility of not having "seen" the jewel on their own, and reduced the chance that the parents would be placed in a position where they were likely to react by defending themselves against the novel perspective.

A central and highly essential spot of blockage centered in this family's ideational sphere was transported back into the fluid interface between ideational and material planes of culture by means of a powerful image. Resilience in family culture appeared to be restored and this set the family free to adapt to future life with a novel perspective.

Subsequent to the therapeutic interventions described so far, the family was responsive to more practically oriented plans in terms of arranging ways for the boy to reenter society without reverting back to his old patterns. At this time, the family's ability to adapt seemed restored. The therapeutic system was now effective when it focused on concrete planning — including schooling and other engagements suitable for a youth of fourteen years in modern Norwegian society. The point here, is that focusing on practical solutions in therapy will work or not work, depending on the cultural context within which the attempts take place. In the family reported on in this paper, *rigid rituals associated with taboo, subverbal, mythical themes prevented any otherwise sensible solutions from taking effect*. When therapy abandoned the concrete solution approach and focused on ways to deflate subverbal myths of destruction, the family was again adaptive in trying out new ways of conducting its life.

A few concluding remarks need to be made about the therapist in this case. The fact that the therapist, to some extent, had joined the familial culture was viewed as a resource. The therapist was joined in consensus with the family, both in terms of defining the problem, and in terms of seeking solutions to the problem. This created a safe base from which potential transitions could be made. Without this safe base, it is doubtful whether the family would have been receptive to the new procedures introduced by the observational team and the supervisor. Without the joining of the therapist with the family, the client system may have felt vulnerable and in need of defending itself against all intrusion from the outside. Furthermore, the fact that the therapist invited the team of colleagues to look in on the situation, was based on his ability to place himself in a meta position, and from that perspective see his own close involvement with the family.

REFERENCES

Byng-Hall, J. (1984). Family scripts. Oslo: Personal communication.

Caspersen, A. (1987). Oslo: Personal communication.

Cirlot, J.E. (1971). *A dictionary of symbols: Translated from Spanish by Jack Sage*, London: Routledge & Kegan Paul.

Cooper, D. (1970). *The death of the family*, New York: Pantheon Books: A division of Random House.

Freud, S. (1955). *Standard edition of the psychological works of Sigmund Freud, Vol. 17*, London: The Hogarth Press.

Henry, J. (1941). *Jungle People: A Kaingang tribe of the highlands of Brazil*, New York: Augustin Publications.

Henry, J. (1956). Homeostasis in a special life situation. In R. Grinker (Ed.), *Toward a united theory of human behavior*, New York: Basic Books.

Henry, J. (1965). *Culture against man*, New York: Random House.

Ibsen, H. (1881). *Gengangere (Ghosts)*, Kobenhavn: Gyldendal.

Levi-Strauss, C. (1966). *The savage mind*, Chicago: The University Chicago Press.

Levi-Strauss, C. (1968). *Structural anthropology, Vol. 16*, London: The Penguin Press.

Levi-Strauss, C. (1985). In E. Leach, & L. Strauss (Eds.), *The structure of myth*, Fontana Press.

Seltzer, W.J. (1984). Treating anorexia nervosa in the somatic hospital: A multisystemic approach. *Family Systems Medicine, 2*, 195-208.

Seltzer, W.J. (1985a). Conversion disorder in childhood and adolescence: A familial/cultural approach. Part I. *Family Systems Medicine, 3*, 261-280.

Seltzer, W.J. (1985b). Conversion disorder in childhood and adolescence. Part II: Therapeutic issues. *Family Systems Medicine, 3*, 397-416.

Seltzer, W.J. & Seltzer, M.R. (1983). Material, myth and magic: A cultural approach to family therapy. *Family Process, 22*, 3-14.

Seltzer, W.J. & Seltzer, M.R. (1987). Culture, leave-taking rituals and the psychotherapist. In O. Van der Hart (Ed.), *Coping with loss*, New York: Irvington Press.

Snorre, S. (1973). *Den yngre Edda*, Oslo: Samlaget.

Turnball, C. (1972). *The mountain people*, New York: Simon & Shuster.

Wallace, A.F.C. (1966). *Religion: An anthropological view*, New York: Random House.

Family Myth, Metaphor
and the Metaphoric Object
in Therapy

Maurizio Andolfi
Claudio Angelo
Vincenzo F. DiNicola (translator)

SUMMARY. In this paper, case illustrations are used to describe how metaphoric objects can be used in therapy to (1) enter into families' shared myths, (2) transmit messages that transcend the literal contents of a family's narrative and bring to light missing elements of the essential plot, and (3) introduce new or previously fragmented information which can lead to new or revised family myths and accompanying interactional behaviors.

THE CONSTRUCTION AND DEVELOPMENT
OF THE FAMILY MYTH

One of the characteristics of myth is that it appears to be located in an intermediate area where reality and history mesh with fantasy to create new situations in which the original elements are randomly used and bound together. Myth therefore becomes the antithesis of journalism. Whereas a news report cannot arbitrarily select from among many pieces of information to describe accurately what has

Maurizio Andolfi, MD, is Scientific Director, Family Therapy Institute of Rome, Italy, and Editor, *Terapia Familiare*. Claudio Angelo, MD, is a teacher at the Family Therapy Institute of Rome. Vincenzo F. DiNicola, MD, is Assistant Professor of Psychiatry, University of Ottawa, Ontario, Canada.

This paper is an elaboration of several parts of Andolfi and Angelo's new book, *Tempo e Mito in psicoterapia familiare* (Turin: Boringhieri, 1987), which is being translated by DiNicola and will be published by Brunner/Mazel, New York.

occurred, myth grows and develops exactly through its "gaps" — missing or incomplete data — and through explanations based on them. In their place come creative acts of fantasy, which introduce a whole series of questions about the great themes of existence such as life, death, survival, love, fear of the unknown and of loneliness. These are the questions to which myth tries to give an answer. In myth, therefore, both the real and the fantastic coexist. Together they contribute to the construction of a reality for human emotional needs.

If we move now from "historical" or "social" myths to family and personal myths, we notice that they also tend to keep in balance a group of opinions and ideas that are very important for the survival of the system in which they develop.

> The term "family myth" refers to a series of fairly well-integrated beliefs shared by all family members, concerning each other and their mutual position in the family life, beliefs that go unchallenged by everyone involved in spite of the distortions which they may conspicuously imply. (Ferreira, 1963, p. 457)

Family myths and individual myths follow the same scheme of construction and are closely intertwined. It seems taken for granted, however, that once formed from the inter-weaving of the various myths of the individuals who are involved with each other, the family myth tends to be maintained unchanged with the more or less conscious "complicity" of each of them. Family myths therefore rest on emotional factors based on attributions of meaning and use contents which have particular relevance in the social and religious context to which they belong and which are found in the construction of popular mythologies.

> The myth offers from the world not an "image" (at least in a reductive sense), but a model of values and of prescriptive functions, as it is through this that mechanisms of reading, of classification, of interpreting reality are launched. From this point of view myth transmits not so much concrete knowledge as a code that allows one to produce knowledge from observa-

tions and interpretations of reality. (Caprettini et al., 1980, p. 680)

Consequently, myth becomes a "matrix of consciousness" (Lemaire, 1984; Lévi-Strauss, 1970, 1973), representing an element of union and a cohesive factor for those who believe in its truth. To create a myth, therefore, means to translate a series of real events and behaviors[1] into a narrative[2] accepted by all, in which each individual can discover a key to reading his own daily experience and the meaning of his life, while feeling at the same time that he is participating with the rest of the group. Individual myths and family myths are therefore closely interconnected and evolve hand in hand.

On the other hand, this restates the problem of the role of the individual in the creation and modification of the myth. The individual finds himself within a circular process whereby he experiences the effects of the myth, while trying at the same time to change its characteristics and its implications.

Stierlin (1978), expanding on concepts developed by Boszormenyi-Nagy and Spark (1973), has written of "delegation," interpersonal processes by which the delegated person can more or less knowingly be the carrier of particular family tasks. These tasks may be real or imagined and imply that "the delegated person, usually an adolescent, is both sent forth and yet bound to the family by the long leash of loyalty" (Simon et al., 1985, p. 83).

This gives us an insight into a kind of *hierarchical organization* of myths in which the individual myth, sometimes without an apparent connection to the family myth, serves to fulfil and to satisfy it. This occurs on two planes—the transverse plane of relations with the current nuclear family and the longitudinal plane of relations with the trigenerational family. For the creation of a myth and the comprehension of its meaning, it proves useful to consider at least three generations. Each individual's expectations of marriage, of children, of work and of life in general become clearer if we examine not only their past experiences, but also their parents' expectations, and how these in turn were motivated by the corresponding expectations in the parents' families of origin. If, for example, a father's hope is for his child to choose a particular profession and achieve a prestigious position and the child tries to adapt to this (or, alternatively, contests it), it is necessary to ask not only what request the child is bearing, but also what other parental demands the father responded to in his own family interactions when he expressed this expectation.

To introduce into descriptions of family myths a historical dimension, as described by various authors (Anderson & Bagarozzi, 1983; Byng-Hall, 1979; Selvini Palazzoli et al., 1978) and to attribute to personal myths, like an individual in the family, a place of prominence in the creation and the transformation of the structure and content of the family myth, we must abandon conceiving of the family system as static and mechanistic, which is evident in the original definition of the family myth by Ferreira (1963). This new dimension brings us to consider myths as structures that are constructed and modified over time. The "original myth" acquires sense only in the light of what is happening now and through its intertwining with the individual myths of various family members, just as all the family members interact within a "narrative" which precedes them. In contrast to a historical event, where every element has its own place in an already defined theme, myth comes together through a series of relations in continual evolution, which constantly change its meaning and create ever new connections or divergences from the original meaning.

Myth develops in the territory of "the unresolved problems of loss, separation, abandonment, individuation, nourishment and deprivation" (Anderson & Bagarozzi, 1983). The plot follows the "ledger of debits and merits" (Boszormenyi-Nagy & Spark, 1973; see Simon et al., 1985, p. 209) within and across generations that establishes the appearance and the evolution of the various family roles that people always relive. These roles which are common in every family history are based on themes of blame, reparation, the search for perfection, and so on. Symbols and metaphors are the building blocks for the construction of myths (Bagarozzi & Anderson, 1982). These building blocks grow around a few principle themes that function as organizers of context and of significance, into which they insert symbolic contents and the personal emotional experiences attached to them.

MYTH AND METAPHOR

If, as we have seen, symbols and metaphors are the building blocks of myths, it will be necessary to see how each family member makes his own and how they are employed in their individual behavior to respond to demands from other generations of the family and to construct alternative myths.

We have said in our last book that, "Metaphor seems to spring from our need to stop the continuous flow of reality in order to possess it, to recapture what we lose of our everyday experience by means of something that resembles it" (Andolfi et al., 1983, p. 93), in the form of images or of behaviors repeated over time. Such images and behaviors can become "the crossroad where situations originally remote from each other intersect" (Andolfi et al., 1983, p. 93), whereby they become generalized, "freed of time and space, valid in any circumstances. Only the patient's personal history determines when and where the symptomatic behavior will occur" (Andolfi et al., 1983, p. 93).

An example of this is provided by the developing child. One way in which the child can make the content of a relationship "his own" is to symbolize it through a series of specific images and behaviors suitable to represent particular aspects of the relationship (such as an emotional attitude of the mother, one of her expressive gestures, or one of her characteristic ways of speaking or behaving). For the child there are no other possibilities of constructing the meaning of the relationship than by breaking it up into behavioral sequences, which are then "frozen" into a series of images or of one or more suitable symbols to capture the most important quality with which to evoke the relationship later.

It is just this we see at work in play, for example, when the child takes the mother's role and constructs scenes in which he repeats her characteristic behaviors. When watching a child or even an adult, one sometimes says, "He (or she) is really just like his (or her) mother (or father)!" This is the recognition of an individual making the relationship "his own" by replaying those "frozen images" with certain movements or mannerisms typical of their parents.

What we have just said refers to a situation in which a relationship that really exists is reproduced or is attempted to be reproduced. Just as often, however, the behavioral metaphor tries to represent "imaginary" relationships or characters who have roles corresponding to "wishes" more or less explicitly expressed by the significant people in one's life. We will try to explain this point with a couple of examples.

In the film "Fanny and Alexander" by the director Ingmar Bergman, there is a scene in which the father of the two children of the title, alerted by screaming at bedtime from the children's room (where they are playing with a magic lantern along with their cousins), suddenly enters the room to restore order. Perceiving the mysterious and magical atmosphere that has been created with the images of the lantern, he promptly enters this mood, taking an old chair and constructing with it a fantastic story that transforms it into a precious object filled with wondrous qualities. In so doing, he effectively uses his skills as an actor (which are rather poor and melodramatic in the theater) in a concrete family situation. The children are fascinated, following his tale raptly, but showing by their stifled laughter now and then that they succeed in maintaining a subtle boundary separating fantasy and reality. The only one who seems to have completely entered the fantasy world of the father's tale to the point of really seeing the old chair as a precious object is Fanny. She is the youngest child who, in the whole scene, does not once move her eyes from what her father is doing.

Shortly after, to test the effect of his story, the father dresses up like a prowler who (not knowing the story) treats the chair as an old, worthless object.

Father: Well, well, well, what is this junk? (*Shaking the chair with scorn*) What kind of chair is this? Huh, it only stands by a miracle! It's ridiculous, it's so ugly I'm scared to sit on it! Ha, ha, ha (*He pretends to sit on it, but he immediately jumps away as if he received an electric shock*) . . . Aaah! Go to the devil! It looks like this blasted chair is trying to bite my behind! Now you're going to get it! (*Picks it up as if to smash it on the floor*)

Fanny (*Screaming, her face excited*)**:** Don't treat it like that!

A long moment of silence occurs, during which the action stops. The father watches Fanny with a sweet and touching look, he places a hand over his chest and sighs as if a tension was suddenly removed. He approaches his daughter who keeps the same excited expression on her face that accompanied her scream and gives her an affectionate caress. With this, the scene concludes.

We find Fanny several times again in the course of the film in the same dreamy mood, but above all with the same attitude of a child who is able to believe in fables and to go through life with a serene faith in the value of objects and the memories that are captured in them. Although this scene represents only a fragment of their family life and a brief glimpse of the relationship that binds Fanny to her father, it is indicative of the way in which an attitude becomes transmitted in the face of reality and in which a family and personal myth is constructed and expressed by the individual's behavior. Fanny is a child who, in her father's expectations, must conduct herself with serene faith and acceptance in her interactions, who always presents herself with a tranquil expression even in the most dramatic circumstances, and who displays openly her own feelings without conflicts or contradictions. All this is expressed in her "mask of gestures" whose features will be shaped by metaphors.

The metaphoric object becomes a pretext for entering into myth, for transmitting a series of messages *that go beyond the content of the story on which it has been constructed* and which enter the arena of relationships and expectations. The object simultaneously becomes a metaphor of the relationship and, when needed, a litmus paper that reveals the contents and, above all, the expectations that reside within it. Applying these observations to what occurred in the scene just described, it is clear at this point that an ordinary chair has been transformed into a completely different and meaningful object of value, acquiring previously unknown qualities. It's equally evident that the relationships between Fanny and the object and between the object and other objects in their "world" have changed. A mythical element has been introduced into their magical expectations which also functions as a prescription for behavior. In this case, however, Fanny does not need to imitate anyone else in the family. In the conduct of her life, she needs to counterbalance the pessimism of her father with her own innocent faith.

The second example we want to report refers to a clinical case. The Estes are a young married couple (the husband is thirty-six and the wife is thirty) living in Northern Italy who asked for marital therapy for the husband's sexual problem (premature ejaculation) which has gradually eroded their relationship. In spite of this, they have had three children, all closely spaced in time. Both of the spouses come from large families — the husband from a family of five children, the wife from a family of four. They met in university, deciding to marry as soon as they finished their studies, which they did.

When the couple comes for their first session, the therapist is immediately struck by a number of contrasts. The wife, who is a physically imposing woman with a wise and calm manner, emanates a feeling of "security" although her facial expression remains vague and her voice now and then seems on the verge of tears. The husband is very precise and refined in his speech and gives the impression of being cultured and self-assured. His movements and his manner, however, are of a depressed person: he constantly has a sad expression on his face, his gestures are slowed, his speech is slow and monotonous, as if talking only to fulfill an obligation, on behalf of someone else. He seems almost to give the message that, even if he is physically present, he is not really there. The overall impression is an atmosphere of "death," of terminal illness, of which both of them are well aware, even if for the occasion they act as if nothing is wrong.

The therapist inquires about their families of origin and discovers that the wife is from a German-Swiss family. She emigrated to Italy following her marriage and she has outwardly adapted so well to her new environment that her spoken Italian does not betray her Swiss origin at all. She seems to be just like any of her husband's friends, with a light Emilian accent. Her parents separated when she was ten years old and she always had to help her mother raise her younger siblings.

Wife: I had practically no youth. I couldn't do what other kids my age did because my mother was very rigid, old-fashioned, and I was forced to work the whole day for the sake of the family after my father left. . . . My father was different, he liked to enjoy himself once in a while, he loved good cooking and sometimes he drank too much. That must have been one of the reasons that my parents decided to separate.

Her father died four years earlier and, remembering her loss, the woman begins to cry:

> I was very attached to him, even if we were never able to talk together. I was more open with my mother. I would go to see him sometimes in Switzerland, in the city where he lived with his new wife and he also came to visit us regularly in Italy.

Therapist: How is it that you had such a close attachment to your father, if you've always been more open with your mother?

Wife: I was never able to explain it . . . . *it was as if I always had to try to figure out whether my father really loved me, if he left us for other reasons although he really loved us.*

We will see shortly what influence this had on her marriage. Let us complete the picture with the husband's family.

The husband's parents are farmers, living in Emilia, a region in Northern Italy situated on a plain, with great expanses of fields and orchards, where the people have strong passions and are considered very sanguine, vital and frank. The husband is the youngest member of his family and was most protected by his mother who seems to expect many things from him that she does not receive. The patient made a pointed statement about this: *"Ever since I was little, I felt my parents and especially my mother breathing down my neck."* The father always mattered very little in the family, he was usually absent and preoccupied with his work in order to "keep up the shack." He was never personally interested in the children and never had any dialogue with them. When the patient was a child, his mother often went to the cemetery, bringing him along to visit the various tombs of family members and friends. These were the only times when she "let herself go," revealing her feelings, mostly of sadness and desertion. At other times, she looked very controlled, superficially cold and incapable of giving affection. "Since I was a child, I felt that my mother expected that I would never abandon her, that I would always be at hand and that she would be able to lean on me." It seems that to a lesser degree this implicit rule holds for the other children as well, to the point that none of them was able to get away from the farm, maintaining the family's patriarchal structure.

Apparently, the only one who broke the rule was the patient when he left home to get married and "to get away from the sort of prison that I felt around me. . . . But since my youth I've felt incapable of facing my problems in life and creating my own space." Now, however, he has recreated his prison in his marriage, especially since his wife, like his mother, expected to have total support from him: "She told me, when we started living together, that she wanted me to promise one thing above all else: *that I would never desert her.*" This feeling of being "caged in" was accentuated after the birth of their children, especially the third, which represented for him the seal of his destiny to work and slave forever merely to survive (he is the only one employed and has a modest salary).

These aspects of the family histories of the two spouses illustrate well to what degree a nonverbal attitude, frozen into facial and bodily gestures can become habitual, almost part of the person's physiognomy. They acquire meaning not only as *metaphors of current relationships*, but also as *metaphors of the family myth which the person bears.*

In the couple of our example, the contrasting features of each spouse are metaphors of their history to be uncoded by the therapist and of the destinies that their respective family myths have assigned them. For the wife, her reassuring calmness and physical "impressiveness" contrast with the ambiguity of her facial expressions and her voice on the verge of tears. For the husband, his precise search for the right word and his rationality contrast with his depressed and lifeless expression. *Their gestures have become a "condensed core" of family rules, around which have clotted all the old expectations of their respective families of origin and their attempts to integrate them into a personal view of life and the world.*

By tracing back the various threads that spread out from this core, to the historical roots of the meanings and the original expectations that have gradually been superimposed on it later, it is possible to reconstruct the plot of the family myth. A key to the plot is in examining the adaptations of the couple and their assigned roles.

The choice of a partner represents a crucial point in everyone's life, because different components converge in that choice. The family "mandate," which is made up of a number of historical events, confronts the individual's expectations which are often confused (since they are underused and often neglected), to make room for the family's expectations (Bowen, 1979; Cigoli, 1983; Framo, 1982; Haley, 1983; Imber-Black, 1986; Sager, 1976; Sluzki, 1978; Whitaker, 1982). In fact, during the whole course of the individual's development in his family of origin, the two needs—personal and familial—have been in constant confrontation and the temporary result depends on *the force and the rigidity* with which the family needs have been imposed on those of the individual, and how much tolerance there is for each individual's personal space. This is especially true during childhood and adolescence, when the individual's dependence on the family places him in an unfavorable position for the full expression of his aspirations.

It is only *at the time of making his selection* that the person finds that he must take responsibility for his actions and to really experience what up to then he has permitted himself to live out only in fantasy, often in opposition to the constraints in his environment. The attempt is always to integrate and to reconcile dissonant elements; that is, to find some kind of compromise that satisfies both the demands of the family and those which in fantasy or in reality oppose them (Dicks, 1967; Nicolò-Corigliano, 1985; Pincus & Dare, 1978). When this is realized, the final product represents a *condensation* of attempts to respond to these numerous demands. The process is essentially comparable to what we see at work in the creation of symptoms which is the point of convergence of different needs and the process of mediation between them. The symptom represents the best compromise, seeking to express the needs adequately and to give them satisfaction.

The qualities attributed by each of the Este spouses to their imaginary partner and to the relationship to be established with him/her should be contrasted with those which, in the interactions with one or the other member of the family of origin, were experienced as negative or problematic. The wife dreamed of marrying not only to finally obtain the autonomy which would permit her to recover what she had lost during her childhood, but also to find a definitive and satisfying solution for her need to be loved and her fear of abandonment. Her husband would have to give her the love, zest for life, and protection that were missing in her family of origin. Instead, she found herself in a situation similar to her mother's in many aspects, mirroring the image of a disappointed woman who feels she must renounce her own aspirations and who sees her children as both her only avenue for gratification and a burden which obliges her to undertake more and móre sacrifices.

The husband hoped to free himself from his "mother's breath" and to be "supported and helped" instead of "doing the supporting." He hoped that his wife would contribute financially to the family and permit him to become independent while providing him with the necessary support. He finds himself instead obliged to respond to her pressing needs for support and to increasing financial and emotional demands, which make him feel imprisoned and suffocated. His dreamed-of freedom has been transformed into a bond from which he must again flee.

Paradoxically, both spouses find themselves more and more in a situation that resembles the one they were in when leaving home, with the same questions and the same unmet needs, each fulfilling a family mandate that places him/her in the very same role, but with a considerable increase in their initial commitments. The husband's symptom symbolizes a kind of seal on all the demands that occur in their new family which are added to all the old ones of their parents.

His premature ejaculation can be "read," in fact, as the condensation of several diverse elements. The impossibility of satisfying his wife seems to symbolize both the persistence of a bond with his mother and his incapacity to respond to a family mandate that would make him function as a "powerful" and conciliating man. On the other hand, despite having fathered three children, his symptom seems to confirm his weakness and his dependence on his wife, who feels justifiably reassured about her own fears of abandonment. In fact, when it comes out during therapy that she experiences her husband's problem as a kind of refusal, it becomes clear that his premature ejaculation makes him afraid to have extramarital sex which might result in the same sexual problem, thus making him stay with her. In this way, their opposing needs find a kind of coexistence and perpetuate their problems without a clear solution.

METAPHOR AND THE METAPHORIC OBJECT
IN THERAPY

The metaphors that families carry can therefore become one of the means which the therapist uses to reconstruct the mythical plot of the family and the roles assigned to each of them. They represent a point of departure for the exploration of this plot, to re-establish a process where initially, only one image appears, frozen in time. In fact, tracing back the threads that lead from current relations to original ones so that the bonds of dependence and attachment will emerge where they will appear only as differences or absences of communications, means bringing to light *the "missing" plot* and identifying the threads, real or imagined to be separated. In some ways, this is the same as giving them different meanings and constructing the outlines of a new story.

In order to do this, the therapist can use not only metaphoric images evoked in him by the way the family's problem is presented, but also by suitable objects which represent them concretely and use them to explore various aspects of the problem. "The choice of the metaphoric object is *an inventive act* with which he introduces a new 'code' which defines and interprets what is happening. This code forms the basis for redefining the relationship among family members" (Angelo, 1981) and between them and their families of origin.

The metaphoric object in therapy does not lead suddenly to an interpretive key to reality which the whole family can grasp at once, but represents a continual stimulus for reading the constantly changing aspects of their reality, and is a potential bearer of new information. It becomes an instrument for the individual to regain some sense of his personal world, often fragmented through family experiences, and a point of departure for the exploration of the mythical contents of family experiences.

The Throne Ritual

Lea Grillo is a woman in her fifties, plump but still attractive, tall and lady-like who has suffered for more than twenty years from depression. For almost half of her life she has been in treatment with an incredible number of neurologists and psychiatrists, trying all kinds of antidepressants and anxiolytics until she has become seriously addicted.

This is her first attempt at family therapy, although her husband Mauro and her two sons, Giacomo (twenty-eight years old, recently married and out of the house) and Luigi (twenty-four), have been fully involved in her drug treatment. Although the motivation for therapy is Lea's depressive state, from the first interactions it is clear that her pharmacological career and her "professional" knowledge about medications and treatment gives her the right to present herself as an absolute authority on the subject, both in her interactions with family members and with therapists. Her intrusiveness, in both her spoken and body language, matches perfectly with the husband's attitude of resignation, who stays motionless to one side, with a vacant stare and the attitude of somebody who "isn't there." The sons, tall and imposing, look like two large watch-dogs, at the service of their mother.

The first attempts of the therapist to somehow rouse the men of the family have a disastrous effect. Whatever they state (and this is already in itself extremely draining for them), gives Lea the chance to rebut and to straighten everything out. The sequence ends unmistakably with the husband even more absent and the sons "curled up" closer to mother's side. Lea's intrusiveness and the state of subjection played by the others is repeated with complementary harmony, without obstacles or pauses. The music is always the same, the "dominant chord" is Lea's illness, who *must* remain the theme around which family life and interactions revolve. Lea speaks of her suffering, crying from time to time as she remembers her episodes of depression, but more with the tone of a dramatic recital, than the real experience of an illness. Her depression seems more like a worn-out dress that Lea has worn for years and that she can no longer take off. In fact, this masks the *real* depression of a woman who is lively and attentive to others but defenceless and unfamiliar to herself. The men of the family present themselves as empty people without interactions among themselves, who take on the semblance of an identity only in their roles as nurse-subjects to Lea.

This is the way in which the family presents itself in the first few sessions of therapy. The therapist feels that opposing the family's rigidity, with their well-rehearsed roles, would be an error that could place him quickly on the list of the many impotent professionals encountered by Lea in the past twenty years. It would be equally mistaken to conclude with a diagnosis of intractability of the case based more on formal criteria than on any meaningful information about the relational and developmental world of the family. Therefore, at this point, the therapist chooses to construct a therapeutic strategy that uses the family script, accentuating the parts played by each individual until they become distinct images charged with meaningful emotions.

The Drug Throne

From the third session.

Therapist: (*Flinging open the door, re-enters with a blue velvet armchair, with a very high back and imposing arms. Turning to the mother*) We have found a chair worthy of you, a veritable throne. (*To the sons*) Would you two "valets" come and take the throne and place it in the center of the room?

Father: (*Surprised*) It's a throne!

Therapist: Yes, it really looks like a throne.

Sons: Is it alright here?

Therapist: (*Turning to the mother, wavers between incredulity and annoyance*) Signora, this throne expresses a lot more, to me . . .

Mother: (*Annoyed*) What does it express?

Therapist: Your situation, much better than that rickety little chair (*pointing to the chair that the lady was sitting on till then*).

Mother: Not at all, as far as I'm concerned.

Therapist: I know, Signora, but as soon as you sit on the throne, we'll be able to understand. . . . You (*turning to the sons*), take your positions again too, here on the floor, at the foot of the throne; I don't think you can give them up so easily.

Mother: (*Sitting solemnly on the throne*) If you tell me to sit here, I'll sit here, but it doesn't feel right (*laughs complacently*).

Father: And where am I?

Therapist: You, I'm sorry to say, are in a different position, more distant, still in the ground, but under it.

Father: Underground? And how am I supposed to get there?

Therapist: You feel like you've been there for at least twenty years, it shouldn't be so difficult now to find the right position here in the session.

The idea of the throne and its appearance in the session produces an abrupt break in the course of therapy which is intended to induce a crisis in the therapeutic system.

The spatial amplification of relations between the members of the family (Lea in her regal position on the throne, her subject-sons at her feet, her husband distant and underground) and between them and the therapist (who is on his feet, walking around the room), allows the therapist to direct the family script better and to introduce links and questions that transform the meaning attributed until then to each role. By placing Lea on the throne, the therapist communicates to the family that in therapy he is the one who assigns parts. What's more, it deprives the patient of the total control that hinders her from getting in touch with her depression and blocks any direct exchange between father and sons.

In the course of the session the throne becomes a *drug throne* which is always reaching higher. As a result, Lea can be regal only in her condition as a chronic patient. If the drugs were removed from under the throne, the support that holds it up would fall. If the throne breaks, perhaps she would not even know if she had been born; or if she was a daughter, a wife, a mother. . . . Therefore to stay on the throne is her only way of "living."

The husband, if he re-emerged from underground might notice that he had married two people—*Lea and the throne*, and that perhaps it is difficult now to choose from which of the two to separate.

The sons cannot imagine a mother without a throne or their lives away from the throne. Through this construction of links and of meaningful relationships, the therapist forcefully introduces the image of the throne into their world of family values. This image becomes a persistent and perturbing stimulus, filled with questions for everybody; an image that will be difficult to refuse, because it has become concrete and tangible in the session. It acts as a "worm" squirming into everybody's mental circuits.

To give the construction of the throne more intensity it is useful to ritualize at home what is acted out in the session. Lea must let herself be equipped by her three men with a chair-throne at home as well. In this way, when she sits on it she will discover how difficult her position really is.

Papa's Throne

Three months later. The brother and sister of the patient are participating in the session.

(The therapist re-enters with a helper who brings the "throne" and places it in the center of the room.)

Father: *(With satisfaction)* This is the throne!

Therapist: You recognize it? *(He then lets Lea sit on the throne, taking her there by hand).*

Lea: *(Sitting down)* But I don't want to stay here anymore!

Therapist: Yeah, I know!

Lea: And, in spite of that, you're going to make me stay here?

Therapist: As long as in your family's mind your father is still on the throne. . . . You will not be able to step down from this throne easily.

Lea: Then my father was on a throne?

Therapist: . . . of drugs! *(Turning to Lea's brother)* Tell me, was your father on a higher or lower throne?

Brother: No, I don't understand this . . .

Therapist: . . . a throne of drugs.

Brother: Yes, I remember that when he had to go to the doctor, we all had to concentrate on him and stop whatever else we were doing . . . what you say is true, though I've never thought of it.

Sister: When he went into the hospital he was happy, because they'd take care of him, watch him. The doctors used to say: "We've never seen such a hypochondriac."

Therapist: What did he defend his throne from?

Sister: He attracted attention . . . in order to feel appreciated. He always talked about his pains. If you told him that he was well, he would be struck dumb.

Therapist: (*Solemnly*) He was a king on a throne of drugs. A king who asks all his subjects to be there at his feet.

Brother: It's true, it's true. . . . Do you remember, Lea . . . **the time he was getting over an illness, he was thirty-five years old then, when he bought an armchair where he said he had to die** (*emphasis added*).

Therapist: (*Turning to Lea*) So your father decided to die on a throne.

Brother: That's what he thought . . . in order to have everybody's admiration.

Therapist: Certainly . . . (*turning to the brother and pointing to Lea*) she's very generously trying to bring your father's project to a conclusion. Look at how regal she is! With that string of pearls. . . . She was born to the throne. . . . A queen. If your father would do a painting . . . she looks like a queen from a Flemish painting.

Lea: (*With an altered tone of voice*) He did a painting of me. A madonna. Dressed as a bride. I was twenty-five years old.

Therapist: (*Turning to the sister*) Did he only do a painting of Lea or did he paint you too?

Sister: No, no, not me.

Therapist: In fact, I don't really see you up there (*pointing to the throne*) at all. You must be someone who takes things into your own hands . . .

Sister: Yes, that's true.

Therapist: The fact is, you wouldn't want to be on a throne!

Sister: No.

Therapist: I understand you!

Lea: (*With anger*) But I don't want to be here either!

Therapist: It isn't possible, it seems made to measure for you. (*Turning to the sister*) What would your father have needed to come down off his throne?

Sister: Respect from his wife . . . it was a question of respect.

Therapist: But did he respect himself? You have told me that he had talent as a painter . . .

Sister: Him? His upbringing was all based on "home, church and state" . . . but very repressive.

Lea: (*With a more authentic tone of voice*) You see, doctor, papa stuttered since he was a child . . . I think he had big problems in his childhood . . . and it bothered me to see mama treating him so badly.

Therapist: I just had a crazy idea: maybe by sitting on papa's chair, for Lea it's a little like being able to stay in his arms . . . (*Turning to the brother and sister*) I would like to give you a task, if you want to keep helping me. At the next session, you must bring me daddy's armchair.

From the fake throne brought in on many occasions by the therapist, in less than five months of therapy, the family has moved on to Lea's father's armchair. Although it is also full of medical implications and a foreboding of death, it nevertheless belongs to the family's affective world. Tracing back together their history made up of rejections and disrespect as well as "magical" expectations of acceptance and confirmation will allow Lea's depression to be put into a developmental framework and to give herself and her family members the possibility of "touching" her. In this way, she will become more understandable and less a chronic patient.

Lea sends signals about where she is headed. Her angry determination to stay alive prevails over her wish to hide behind drugs. For the first time she agrees to admit herself to a hospital to get detoxi-fied and, more important, to let herself be "guided" by her hus-band in her treatment program at home. The road to freedom from this monarchy is still long, but at least a path to follow is visible. The throne will be used again in the sessions in the months to come. Lea will be able to *choose* where to sit and the others will also be able to choose where to place themselves.

Staying on the throne or choosing an ordinary chair will then have very different implications, as will whether or not to remain "subjects" at the foot of the throne or "underground." Everyone's habitual responses will be replaced by more awkward but unques-tionably more lively movements and attitudes. They will begin a phase of discoveries. The need for attention, for example, so long monopolized by Lea and denied to the others, will be sought by everyone. Even Lea's husband, Mauro, will finally be able to sit on the throne, which he will call the "throne of importance."

Alternating thrones and their occupants teaches the family first how to free themselves from monarchies and later from the therapist in order to face life's difficulties on their own.

NOTES

1. In our reading, the fact that myth is based at least partly on real elements distinguishes myth from fable.

2. The narrative constitutes the formal structure in which myth is organized, introduced by those who construct it over time with both real and fantastic ele-ments. The narrative is one of the means through which myth is handed down. In fact, it can also be transmitted implicitly through the assignment of roles, expecta-tions, values attributed to actions, and so on.

REFERENCES

Anderson, S.A. and Bagarozzi, D.A. (1983). The use of family myths as an aid to strategic therapy. *Journal of Family Therapy, 5*, 145-154.

Andolfi, M., Angelo, C., Nicolo-Corigliano, A., and Menghi, P. (1983). *Behind the family mask: Therapeutic change in rigid family systems*. New York: Brun-ner/Mazel.

Angelo, C. (1981). The use of the metaphoric object in family therapy. *American Journal of Family Therapy, 9*, 69-78.

Bagarozzi, D.A. and Anderson, S. (1982). The evolution of family mythological systems: Considerations for meaning, clinical assessment, and treatment. *Journal of Psychoanalytic Anthropology, 5*, 71-90.

Boszormenyi-Nagy, I. and Spark, M. (1973). *Invisible loyalties: Reciprocity in intergenerational family therapy*. New York: Harper & Row.

Bowen, M. (1979). *Dalla famiglia all 'individuo*, edited by Andolfi, M. and De Nichilo, M. Rome: Astrolabia.

Byng-Hall, J. (1979). Reediting family mythology during family therapy. *Journal of Family Therapy, 1*, 2-14.

Caprettini, G., Ferraro, G., and Filoramo, G. (1980). Mythos/logos. In: *Encyclopedia*, Vol. 9: 660-689, Turin: Einaudi.

Cigoli, V. (Ed.) (1983). *Terapia familiare. L'orientamento psicoanalitico*. Milan: Angeli.

Dicks, H. (1967). *Marital tensions. Clinical studies toward a psychological theory of interaction*. London: Routledge & Kegan Paul.

Ferreira, A. (1963). Family myth and homeostasis. *Archives of General Psychiatry, 9*, 457-463.

Framo, J. (1982). *Explorations in marital and family therapy*. New York: Springer.

Haley, J. (1973). *Uncommon therapy: The psychiatric techniques of Milton H. Erickson, M.D.* New York: W.W. Norton & Company.

Imber-Black, E. (1986). Odysseys of a learner. In D. Efron (Ed.) *Journeys: Expansion of the strategic/systemic therapies*. New York: Brunner/Mazel.

Lemaire, J.G. (1984). La realite informe, le mythe structure. *Dialogue, 2.*

Lévi-Strauss, C. (1970). *The raw and the cooked*. Translated by J. Weightman and D. Weightman. Vol. I in Introduction to a Science of Mythology Series. New York: Harper & Row.

Lévi-Strauss, C. (1973). *From honey to ashes*. Translated by J. Weightman and D. Weightman. Vol. II in Introduction to a Science of Mythology Series. New York: Harper & Row.

Nicolo-Corigliano, A. (1985). La relazione de coppia in gravidanza. *Crescita, 12.*

Pincus, L. and Dare, C. (1978). *Secrets in the family*. New York: Pantheon Books.

Sager, C. (1976). *Marriage contracts and couple therapy*. New York: Brunner/ Mazel.

Selvini Palazzoli, M., Boscolo, L., Cecchin, G., and Prata, G. (1978). *Paradox and counterparadox*. New York: Jason Aronson.

Simon, F.B., Stierlin, H., and Wynne, L.C. (1985). *The language of family therapy: A systemic vocabulary and sourcebook*. New York: Family Process Press.

Sluzki, C. (1978). Marital therapy from a systems perspective. In T. Paolino and B. McCrady (Eds.), *Marriage and marital therapy: Psychoanalytic, behavioral and systems theory perspectives*. New York: Brunner/Mazel.

Stierlin, H. (1978). *Delegation und familie*. Frankfurt: Suhrkamp.

Whitaker, C. (1982). From psychoanalysis to family therapy. In J. Neill and D. Kniskern (Eds.), *From psyche to system: The evolving therapy of Carl Whitaker*. New York: Guilford.

Myths and Rituals:
Anthropological Views
and Their Application
in Strategic Family Therapy

Onno van der Hart
Eliezer Witztum
Anna de Voogt

SUMMARY. Myth is often used in family therapy as a synonym for erroneous belief or fallacy which preserves a distorted reality of the family, and the concept of ritual is commonly limited to well-defined behavioral prescriptions. Anthropologists, however, emphasize the positive functions of myth and agree on both the ceremonial and symbolic nature of rituals. They also provide a framework for relating the two concepts. This paper presents three anthropological theories of functions of myth which seem relevant to family therapists, and provides a working definition of ritual. Using a case example, it proposes a bifocal model of family therapy which connects the two concepts to two levels of culture, i.e., its ideational plane and its material plane, and helps to integrate therapeutic interventions at both levels.

Anthropologists and sociologists generally agree that myths are sacred narratives (cf. Dundes, 1984a). In family therapy, however, myths have been perceived differently. Ferreira (1963) defined

Onno van der Hart is affiliated with the Department of Psychiatry, Free University, Amsterdam, Netherlands. Eliezer Witztum is affiliated with the Jerusalem Mental Health Center-Ezrath Nashim, Jerusalem, Israel. Anna de Voogt is affiliated with the Dercksen Center for Mental Health, Amsterdam, Netherlands. Correspondence should be directed to Dr. van der Hart, Department of Psychiatry, Hospital of the Free University, P.O. Box 7057, 1007 MB Amsterdam, Netherlands.

family myths as a series of fairly well integrated beliefs shared by family members concerning each other and their mutual position in family life. These beliefs go unchallenged by everyone in spite of the reality distortions which they may conspicuously imply. Ferreira and others seem to use myth as a synonym for an erroneous belief or fallacy, which preserves a distorted family reality (cf. Byng-Hall, 1973; Pillari, 1986; Selvini Palazzoli et al., 1977; Stierlin, 1973). It follows, therefore, that such erroneous beliefs are to be corrected. One strategy to alter such organized belief systems, is to use ritual prescriptions. In family therapy, the concept of ritual is used in many different ways but unfortunately its symbolic nature has been virtually ignored. Anthropologists, however, agree upon the importance of the ceremonial and symbolic nature of myths and rituals.

Our goal in this paper is to elaborate on the symbolic significance of myths and rituals and to show how they can be used in family therapy. Anderson and Bagarozzi (1983) have done some work in this area as have Laird (1984) and van der Hart (1983). Seltzer and Seltzer (1983) have also offered a framework utilizing myth and ritual in family therapy.

A BIFOCAL MODEL OF FAMILY CULTURE

In modern anthropology, social groups such as tribes and families are thought to consist of two interrelated structures; the social and the cultural (Geertz, 1973). Tennekes (1979) refers to them as the social order and the symbolic order. Seltzer and Seltzer (1983) call them the material plane and the ideational plane of a culture. The terminology carries with it the notion that the way people interact with each other is culturally determined.

The material plane of family culture is seen in the family's observable behaviors (e.g., rituals, repetitive patterns). The ideational plane, on the other hand, is nonmaterial and nonobservable (e.g., beliefs, values, and affects shared wholly or in part by family members). It provides the contexts for myths by defining various situations, by prescribing role relationships, by permitting the expression of certain feelings and opinions and by offering a consensus of meaning by which family members interpret their experiences and conduct their behavior (Geertz, 1973). The material plane concerns, in Geertz's terms, the form this action takes, the actual existing network of social relationships. Both planes have their own dynamics and imply each other. These two planes stand in opposition to each other in a dialectic— and often tense— relationship to each other (Murphy, 1971; Tennekes, 1979; Seltzer & Seltzer, 1983).

Myths belong to the ideational plane of culture, and rituals to the material plane. Because of their symbolic nature, rituals are also intimately connected with the ideational plane, i.e., to the group's shared constructs of reality.

ANTHROPOLOGICAL AND RELATED VIEWS ON MYTH

The narrative quality of myth distinguishes it from a general idea or set of ideas, such as a cosmology. This narrative quality may be more or less developed. Waardenburg (1980) distinguishes explicit myths which are fully developed stories, from implicit myths, which consist of meaningful, but not fully developed elements of a potential story. While perhaps not all anthropologists would consider the later to be myths, we think that Waardenburg's distinction is of value for families and the practice of family therapy where implicit myths are most often emphasized. One example of what we call an implicit family myth is demonstrated by a woman's statement concerning her spouse: "My husband should be spared: he has already gone through so much." Another example can be seen in this description of a couple's courtship: "We met in Auschwitz." In fact, it was their mothers who had actually met while they were in Auschwitz during WWII.

It is widely held that the sacred quality and the reference to origins and transformations distinguish myths from legends and other types of folktales. According to this viewpoint, most narratives offered by family members about key elements of family structure and process could not be considered myths. However, while accepting the narrative quality of myth, Kirk (1970, 1972) concludes (in a critical review of the literature dealing with myths and myth making) that there is no one definition of myth. Myths differ widely in their meaning and in their social functions. Kirk opposes the definition of myth as being a sacred narrative, because not all myths are concerned with gods and/or religion. He believes that traditional oral tales constitute the only safe basis for a broad definition of myth. In line with this orientation, we limit the concept of family myth to shared traditional oral tales told by the family and its members about the family and its members.

Theory

Theories about the functions of myths were proposed as early as the 6th century B.C. Different disciplines have emphasized different meanings and functions, and these theories often overlap and complement one another (cf. Honko, 1972). Cohen (1969) identified 7 theoretical explanations for the development of myths. Three of these are particularly relevant for family work. These are: (1) Myths serve to explain inexplicable phenomena; (2) Myths develop in order to create and maintain social solidarity and group cohesion; and (3) Myths come about in order to legitimize social institutions and practices.

Modifications of Myths

When changes occur in social institutions and practices — i.e., at the material plane of culture — and the myths which legitimize the previous state of affairs do not fit any longer, then according to van Baaren (1972), the myth will not disappear. On the contrary, to prevent loss of function or total disappearance, the myth will be changed in a way that will allow it to be maintained. Thus, the myth is adapted to the new situation, armed to withstand a new challenge.

An intriguing example given by van Baaren concerns Tahiti, when it was still governed by kings. Change of dynasties was not unknown, and because the noble houses claimed descent from divine beings, their genealogies were of importance to legitimize a claim to the throne. Certain myths were recited (by priests) at important festivals. It was of the utmost importance that this be done without error. Any priest who committed a mistake could be executed. In this way, the myth was preserved intact. When dynasties changed, however, the existing "traditional" myth was no longer in accordance with the new political situation. The priests, therefore, had to make small unobtrusive changes every time they recited the myth, till its text was wholly adapted to the new situation. Officially, the myth was not changed. Van Baaren concludes, that a central characteristic of myth is its tendency to undergo change rather than to disappear. When there is a conflict between mythical and worldly reality, it is most often the myth that changes.

This last statement may seem comforting to family therapists, who deal frequently with analogous conflicts. However, they should also take heed of the fact that these traditional myths were very subtly changed over time and never confronted directly. Families entering therapy usually have not made changes (e.g., leaving home of a young adult) at the material plane of their culture. They are usually experiencing pressure from inside or outside the system to do so. We expect that these families initially try to solve such developmental problems by taking refuge in existing family myths which explain and protect the threatened status quo. This explains the resistance they exhibit when confronted with direct assaults on a prevailing myth.

Conclusion

The three theoretical views noted above may be seen as emphasizing different functions of myths. Some myths are more concerned with explaining inexplicable phenomena, while others may be geared primarily to maintaining group solidarity, or to legitimizing social institutions and practices. Family therapists should become familiar with the purpose of a particular family myth and realize that in all likelihood, it will not disappear. The best that can be hoped for is modification through some indirect means.

DEFINING RITUAL

There is a wealth of anthropological literature dealing with rituals, which could be of considerable value to family therapists. Ritual is a complex phenomenon. Traditionally, anthropologists focused on the magical and religious rituals of so-called primitive societies, in which ancient people communicated with their gods (cf. Durkheim, 1915). This view is reflected in an arbitrary example of a contemporary definition, which states that ritual is "a system of religious or magical ceremonies or procedures, frequently with special forms, vocabulary, and usually associated with important occasions or actions" (Drever, 1965).

However, many modern anthropologists and sociologists disagree with the exclusive magico-religious character of rituals, and consider secular rituals as equally important (cf. Bossard & Boll, 1950; Douglas, 1966; Moore & Myerhoff, 1977).

Another problem with Drever's definition is that it ignores the symbolic aspect of ritual, which anthropologists such as Turner (1967, 1978) and Tennekes (1982) consider to be essential. Certain ritual acts are symbolic acts, which have an expressive character. Their right of existence is derived from the "message" they represent. Some of these symbolic acts consist of the manipulation of symbols. Thus, they are analogical actions: the way in which one treats the symbol is analogical to the way in which one would like to treat that which is symbolized (Skorupski, 1976; van der Hart, 1988a).

The symbolic aspect of ritual is also conspicuously absent in most definitions family therapists provide. For instance, Selvini Palazzoli (1974) emphasized the prescribed nature of rituals and ignored their symbolic value—which is nevertheless very much present in her case examples. One example concerns the family in which the two and a half-year-old daughter became anorectic after her baby brother died in the hospital. She had not been informed of this fact. The parents were instructed to tell her about his death and about the funeral and, together with her, to solemnly bury his baby clothes in their garden (Selvini Palazzoli, Boscolo, Gecchin & Prata, 1974). Our own definition is an attempt to include this symbolic aspect. For us, *rituals are prescribed symbolic acts that must be performed in a certain way and in a certain order, and may or may not be accompanied by verbal formulas* (van der Hart, 1983). We would add today that these prescribed symbolic acts are central parts of complex rituals, which are "open" to improvisation and modification (cf. Moore & Myerhoff, 1977; Tennekes, 1982).

THERAPEUTIC MYTHS AND RITUALS

Many authors believe that there always exists an intimate relationship between myth and ritual (Fontenrose, 1959; Gaster, 1954; Kluckholn, 1942; Leach, 1954). According to some, myth is but an offspring or projection of ritual; according to others, ritual is but a subsequent enactment of myth. In the field of family therapy, Bagarozzi and Anderson (1982) adopt this view.

Many myths and rituals are indeed associated. However, there also exist myths which are unaccompanied by any ritual performances, and many rituals cannot be seen as enactments of myths (De Langhe, 1958; Kirk, 1970).

The area where anthropologists usually find a close connection between myth and ritual is in the realm of medicine (i.e., affliction and misfortune) (Kluckholn, 1942; Levi-Strauss, 1963; Turner, 1968; Munn, 1973). During the first stage of the healing process, the negative experiences of the patient are recounted in terms of the myth. The myth tells how the accident, the affliction, or the illness came about and why it remains. It is the medium through which the complaints are given expression in a symbolic manner. The myth is not only a story which explains what went wrong, etc., it also points out the way to restore the person to a previous state of health.

In the second stage the ritual actions are performed by the healer, other members of the community, and the patient. These symbolic actions dispel or transform the negative images which were given expression in the original mythical story (Munn, 1973). They enact transformations of the patient's inner experiences and of the social relationships in which he is an integral component. Thus, we find in the complex of healing myth and ritual all the elements and functions of myth mentioned before: the narrative element, the explanatory function, the function of legitimizing social practices (i.e., the healing ritual), and the function of fostering social solidarity and cohesion.

According to Frank (1973), modern psychotherapy is based on a myth which includes an explanation of illness and health, deviancy and normality. In traditional societies the healing myth is compatible with the cultural world view shared by patient and therapist;

usually, this is a religious world view. Modern therapeutic myths differ from traditional myths in that they are secular and fragmentary. They make no references to prehistoric times, and supernatural beings play no part in them. Strategic therapists usually endeavor to adapt themselves to the world view of the family.

A few authors state that modern psychotherapy can, by itself, be seen as a ritual (e.g., Siggins, 1983; De Tempe, 1987). Family therapy, for instance, has been described as a transitional ritual for the family (Kobak & Waters, 1984). Haley (1973) regards the treatment of the adolescent who cannot leave home as an initiation ceremony. The view we advocate here is that *all the interventions therapists make should be made in terms of the therapeutic myth they have constructed around the presenting problems. The therapeutic activities that family members are asked to perform should be seen as steps towards the transformation of the myth.* For instance, by performing a certain transition ritual, the family is now correctly making the previously unsuccessful transition from one life cycle stage to the next, thereby "restoring normal life" (Ter Horst, 1977).

TOWARDS A BIFOCAL MODEL OF FAMILY THERAPY INTERVENTIONS

In order to incorporate the concepts of family myth and therapeutic myth into a model of family therapy, one must include; both the material plane and the ideational plane of family culture, the family's cultural system, and the therapist's therapeutic myths. In treating families which are relatively open to change, our focus is directed towards changes at the material plane, i.e., the modification of actual interaction patterns in the family. Interventions directed at the ideational plane of family culture — mainly reframing and relabeling — are seen as adjuncts (cf. Lange & van der Hart, 1983). However, when treating severely dysfunctional family systems which are less open to change, we direct our interventions — at least in the initial stage of treatment — more at the ideational plane of family culture. Regardless of the plane of family culture we emphasize, we understand that family therapy always addresses both planes simultaneously. We propose the following treatment model, which not only incorporates family therapy techniques directed at different levels, but also shows how family and therapeutic myths—both explicit and implicit—form an integral part of the overall treatment approach.

A. Interventions at the Ideational Plane of Family Culture

1. *Elaborating existing family myths*. This is the technique used to help family members develop implicit myths into explicit family myths. As a rule, we look for those myths which explain the origin of the illness of the identified patient or the family misfortune, and/or legitimize the current affairs in the family. When such a family myth does not seem to tell the whole story, we are inclined to coach family members — usually the parents — to elaborate related individual myths which they brought into the family (cf. Bagarozzi & Anderson, 1982). Sometimes the parents' stories about their own difficult or even traumatic experiences seem to be the missing link in the mythology of a current family complication.

2. *Presenting the therapeutic myth*. From all available material, including family mythology and other historical data, the therapist constructs an explanatory narrative about how the present problematic state came into being and continues to exist. This is done in such a way that it offers the best possible perspective towards change, but also takes into full account the possible pitfalls. Presenting the therapeutic myth to the family means substituting it for the existing family myth (cf. Janet, 1935).

A related technique is the telling of a metaphoric story or anecdote about another family. Here, the therapeutic myth is presented in an indirect manner.

3. *Relabeling and reframing*. These are well-known techniques, directed at changing the perceptions of the family members and presenting a different view on the presenting problems. Relabeling often takes the form of substituting the family's negative connotations of symptomatic behavior or dysfunctional interaction patterns with more positive ones. When, by relabeling, a completely new frame of reference is introduced, we speak of reframing. A beauti-

ful example is provided by Papp (1983) who redefined the "illness" of an anorectic girl as a hunger strike serving the purpose of remaining pappa's little boy because this father felt left out in the family consisting only of women.

Relabeling and reframing were originally our main interventions at the ideational plane of family culture, often used as an introduction to prescribing the symptom or the system. However, we learned to view these techniques as presenting implicit therapeutic myths; i.e., as meaningful but not fully developed elements of potential stories. Implicit myths have explanatory value, they often stress family cohesion, and when used as an introduction to symptom or system prescription legitimize existing family practices. However, their power can be greatly enhanced when they are integral parts of explicit therapeutic myths. As Janet (1947) mentioned, the ideas that myths contain, when presented as narratives, provide satisfaction to the imagination. The family members gain an understanding of their problems and, eventually, their solutions. They also feel understood.

B. Interventions at the Material Plane of Family Culture

There exists a wide variety of interventions that can be used to change behavior and modify dysfunctional interaction patterns (cf. Hoffman, 1980; Minuchin & Fishman, 1981; Papp, 1983; Lange & van der Hart, 1983). In working with highly resistant families, we tend to prescribe rituals or give ritualized assignments. The timing of such prescriptions is crucial for their success. We distinguish the following uses of rituals (cf. van der Hart, 1983; Laird, 1984).

1. *The prescription of one-time rituals.* Transition rituals help families to mark and celebrate the transition from one state — e.g., one stage in their life cycle — to another. Such rituals need not always be designed and prescribed by the therapist. Families can sometimes be coached to negotiate their own rituals. Transition rituals can be a very powerful means of transforming family myths which explain and legitimize existing states or conditions.

2. *The prescription or modification of repeated rituals.* Such rituals are often family rituals (e.g., bedtime rituals, weekend rituals)

which take place at one particular stage of the family cycle. Developing such rituals is especially helpful for underorganized or disengaged families. Changing them may be desirable when they are experienced by some family members as being too rigid, constraining or repressive.

Comments

Keeping this model in mind helps us to integrate interventions at different levels, i.e., at the material and ideational planes of family culture. Interventions at the material plane (e.g., ritual prescriptions) are defined in terms of the ideational plane by using therapeutic redefinitions of the presenting problem. These redefinitions do not stand on their own, but form an integral part of the therapeutic myth, which relates how these problems came into being and why they continue to exist. This therapeutic myth is a replacement for the family myth. With families that are primarily locked at the ideational plane, it is necessary to first elaborate the relevant family myths and then to replace them with an explicit therapeutic myth.

As an extensive illustration, we did not choose a "perfect" case example, but rather one which exemplifies, in our opinion, what not to do and what to do when the identified problem is related to a family culture which is primarily locked at the ideational plane.

A MATTER OF LIFE AND DEATH

Ronald, a 30-year-old psychology student and the eldest of seven children, was referred to a psychiatric day-hospital after he had made an aggressive suicide attempt. On the day his girl friend left him, he plunged a kitchen knife into his abdomen – an act which was later described by his family as "hara-kiri." After major surgery, he was in a coma for three days. When he woke up, he recovered rather quickly. He was then transferred to the psychiatric ward. After two months, he was referred to a day hospital. On admission to the day hospital, he was depressed. He talked mainly about his shame, worthlessness, indecisiveness and feelings of despair when he thought about his future. The intake worker believed that the main issue was unresolved mourning, not only with regard to the fact that his girlfriend had left him, but especially with regard to his mother's death which occurred when he was eleven. In addition, his relationship with his stepmother seemed problematic. Thus family therapy was recommended.

Description of the Family

The family met the therapist and her two colleagues who were part of the therapeutic team. The therapist used the first two sessions to become acquainted with the family, to learn its history, and to learn more about how the family members viewed their deceased mother. She was struck by the fact that the family members described the mother and Ronald in similar ways: both had been real "worriers," both were indecisive, and both were very ambivalent about the importance of status.

The family consisted of Father, Stepmother (a younger sister of Father's first wife), three sons and four daughters — all children of the first marriage. Father was a businessman who had recently retired after a minor stroke. Stepmother had moved into the house on the day that Father's first wife had died while giving birth to the eighth child. Stepmother had come to help her with the delivery. After her sister died, she decided to stay in order to help out the family. One year later she married Father, and she became "Mama" for the children. All seven children had finished college and were either working or in graduate school. All of them had left home and, except for Ronald and his eldest sister Judy, all were either married or engaged.

The First Family Myth

In the subsequent team discussion, the team attempted to construct the family myth which the family seemed to have presented: It was a large, happy family, and all the family members became even more happy when Mother was expecting another child. On the night of the delivery, Mother's youngest sister (who was fond of children and fond of her sister) came to help. Then something terrible happened. Both the beloved mother and the longed for baby died in childbirth. The family was terribly upset after this tragic event. But life had to go on, and fortunately, Mother's sister was willing to stay to help the family out. All were very grateful to her, and although she was different than Mother in some ways, they got along together quite well. One year after Mother's death, Father and Mother's sister decided to marry. There was a big, happy wedding, which no one would ever forget.

Fortunately, Mama was more practical than Mother and made some improvements in the family rules and rituals. For example, Ronald had held a special position in the family. He was the eldest and a gifted child, and therefore carried many "adult responsibilities." He had been a great help and support to Mother, was very much like her, but had quarreled a great deal with her, too. Mama felt this was because he was overburdened and in need of support. Therefore, she relieved him of his "adult tasks," so that he could study more and develop his talents.

When Ronald went to college, he found a girlfriend to whom he could be helpful and supportive. But when, during his stressful residency year, he needed her support, she failed to provide this. They began to quarrel a great deal, and finally, his girlfriend left him. The family believed that he was overburdened and in need of support, and this was why he attempted suicide.

The Beginning of a Therapeutic Myth

In a team discussion before the end of the second session, the therapists thought that the entry of Mother's sister into the family was not as smooth as the family myth indicated. They also felt that mourning was a much more difficult issue for the family members than the myth suggested. It seemed that the myth's main function was to legitimize the way in which the family was functioning, especially the fact that Mother's sister had taken Mother's place and had changed the family rules and rituals. The team tentatively called the family myth *The Family Savior*.

Ronald apparently accepted his role as the family member who was most like Mother. He also seemed to be the one who most desperately tried to keep her memory alive. However, like the other family members, he had to keep his feelings about her death and the fact that somebody else had taken her place hidden. The team believed that after Mother's death, Ronald still felt a loyalty to her. He tolerated Mama's "improvements and support," but internalized his rage.

In the relationship with his girlfriend, roles were reversed, and he could not tolerate being dependent upon her and in need of her support. When she abandoned him, this loss reactivated his unresolved feelings of loss and rage about the change of roles made by Mama. This rage was manifested in his attempt at "hara-kiri."

The team believed that telling the family their hypotheses, at this stage of treatment would be wrong for two reasons. First more evidence to support this hypothesis was needed. Second, this story would be a direct challenge to the family's myth. Instead, an intervention was devised which used only part of the therapeutic myth.

The First Intervention

At the end of the second session, the therapist told the family that the team was impressed by the fact that Ronald had taken so many characteristics of his late mother. They believed that he was trying to keep her memory alive, but they were not sure why he felt this was necessary. The therapist then invited the family to further explore this issue in the next session which took place four weeks later.

The Second Family Myth

Father called before this session to inform the therapist that he and his wife would not come, since the previous session had been too stressful for her. All seven children showed up, however. It was a loaded session. Ronald and his sister Judy, the second oldest, explained how they had always been unable to accept their aunt — i.e., their stepmother — as a real mother. Silently they had hated their stepmother, and they had often struggled with the question of why Father had ever married her. "Stepmother" was a taboo word around the house. The children had to call their aunt "Mama." They recalled memories of how she changed many family rituals and rules, which had been instituted by their mother. To justify those changes, Mama had used criticisms of their mother. She told stories about her which were always negative and made only one conclusion possible: "Mama was a better mother than their own mother had ever been."

None of the children had ever believed this, but none of them had ever said so. All shared feelings of deep respect for her. She had given up everything for them, but they did not like her very much. When the therapist asked them what they feared if they were to share their true feeling, they all agreed that "It would be the end for Mama. Her world would collapse, her life would be useless and meaningless for her." Kitty, the youngest, age 20, added: "She has nothing else. This is all she has in life."

The Evolving Therapeutic Myth

In the ensuing team discussion, the therapists were tempted to regard the childrens' story as the "true family history," which was covered up by the previously related family myth. However, they were soon able to see both as competing family myths. We labelled the children's myth "The Bad Stepmother." The dominant myth — the parents' myth — celebrated Mama as the good mother, and legitimized her life style. The children's myth celebrated Mother and honored her contributions to the family.

The children saw the dominance of the parents' myth as a matter of life and death for their stepmother. However, keeping his mother's memory alive was also a matter of life and death for Ronald.

We were aware that both myths were not completely incompatible, since the children had expressed feelings of respect for Mama. We believed that the family had the resources to integrate both versions into one family myth; one that could be shared by all members; one that would lead to modifications of family rules and rituals and would allow for the needs and preferences of all family members. We decided that the best way to accomplish this task was to confront both family myths directly using the same kind of dramatic language that had prevailed in the session.

The Second Intervention

When the therapist returned, she told the children this:

The team has been greatly moved and shocked by your stories. What we found especially shocking was the clarity of the answer to our previous question, i.e., why did Ronald feel it necessary to keep the memory of Mother alive. Now we realize that this is a matter of life and death. If the family was to uncover these feelings that there has been only one real Mother and that Mama is a good stepmother and aunt, it would be the end of Mama. Her world would fall apart, her life would be meaningless. If the family continues to hide feelings, as it has been doing for the past 20 years, then Ronald is the only one who sees to it that Mother will not be forgotten, the only one who safeguards this reality. However, by trying to end his life, Ronald has shown that this task has become too much for him. He cannot live with the dominant family myth, and he cannot find support for his own myth.

So the terrible dilemma all of you face is, either Ronald must die or Mama. Now we understand how terrifying your dilemma is. Therefore we think that the goal of future sessions should be to explore with you whether there is a way out of this dilemma or not

Upon hearing the message, Ronald burst into tears. Judy became furious with the therapists, because of what she saw as a rather quick, one-sided conclusion. She felt blackmailed by the team's idea that Ronald's suicide attempt was in this way linked to the family, and she accused the team of making Ronald into a "victim of the family instead of emancipating him." The two younger brothers were moved and thought what the therapist had just said was essential. The three younger sisters cried out that they all had learned to live with the myth, so why not Ronald? The therapist ended the session by inviting the whole family for the next appointment.

The Planning of a Family Ritual

After this session, the team discussed the future course of treatment. It seemed important to integrate the two family myths into one and to utilize the fact that the children had deep respect for Mama. The challenge was to find a way in which the family could both honor and respect Mama and commemorate their beloved Mother. The therapists' aim for the next session was to try and develop (together with the children) a ritual which would serve both purposes. Things went differently, however.

Again, in the fourth session, only the children showed up. They told the therapist that after the previous session, which had greatly moved them, they had gone out to dinner. At the dinner table, they had practiced various ways of discussing the contents of the session with their father and stepmother. Finally, the three younger daughters went home and had told their parents everything that had happened in the session. Father was sympathetic and understanding. Mama, however, was less sympathetic and more despondent, but "she had not collapsed!" The three girls said it had been less difficult than they had expected. Afterwards, all children felt very relieved, but Mama seemed sad and Father was very concerned about her. However, the children no longer understood why they had been so moved by the previous therapy session. At this point, Ronald announced that he had decided to start to work and to study again, and to discontinue family therapy.

The Evolving Therapeutic Myth and Its Consequences

In the ensuing team discussion, the therapists concluded that the previous intervention had triggered a great deal of support for Ronald from his siblings. The children had pulled together to attack the parents' myth and to express their hidden feelings. Although this had relieved them, it depressed Mama. Moreover, it created another situation in which Ronald felt dependent and pushed to accept help. This enraged him. If Ronald were to continue to accept help from his siblings, this would undermine his role in the family as the eldest, gifted strong child, who had to solve his own problems and still be his parents' helper. On the other hand, if he refused help, he would be alone and without support.

The dilemma for the therapists was similar: any therapeutic "help," which Ronald still seemed to need, might have adverse affects. Therefore, it was decided to explain this dilemma to Ronald and his siblings, to bring family therapy to an end, to discharge Ronald from the day hospital, and to offer him a total of ten individual aftercare sessions. Ronald would be asked to help the therapist to not help him and to warn her if he noticed she was showing too much readiness to help.

Follow-Up

Upon hearing this plan, Ronald said he felt really understood, and he recognized this dilemma as a core pattern in his life. He and his siblings agreed to the plan. After discharge, he returned for ten individual sessions and gradually improved.

Follow-up three years later revealed that Ronald had done well. He had quit his psychology studies and had gone into computer science. He was proud of his newly-found job in this field. He had found a new apartment and was dating a new girlfriend. He told us that his stepmother had been depressed for three months after his discharge. Lately, he was feeling closer to her and his father than before and during therapy.

DISCUSSION

1. The Two Stages of the Myth-Ritual Complex

This case example illustrates the first stage of the myth-ritual complex, which, according to Frank (1973) underlies both traditional healing practices and modern therapeutic approaches. This stage, belonging to the ideational plane of culture, consists essentially of developing a narrative account of how the affliction or illness came about and why it still persists. In the present example, the existing family myths were first made explicit, then the therapeutic myth was constructed and presented.

The second stage of the healing complex traditionally consists of ritual actions which are intended to heal the illness or to solve the problems by use of a therapeutic myth. As we mentioned earlier, in modern family therapy, this includes all the interventions directed at the material plane of the family culture — some of these interventions also take the form of rituals, which because of their symbolic nature are also strongly connected with the ideational plane. In the present case example, this stage was not developed but a ritual could have been included.

The two stages of the healing complex should be viewed as a rather abstract model of traditional and modern treatment approaches. In reality, treatment does not consist of two clearly distinguished stages but rather of a continuous interchange, a dialectical interaction between interventions at both ideational and material planes. As this case illustrates, treatment starts generally with the elaboration of family and therapeutic myths and is then followed by interventions at the material plane. However, a process of looping and feedback involving both levels evolves over time.

2. From Family Myth to Therapeutic Myth

Telling the story right — i.e., with a beginning, middle, and an end, and taking into account the actual feelings of both the narrator and the audience — is not an easy feat (cf. Janet, 1929). For example, in many cases, families do not present a fully developed explicit myth, rather, they offer a series of loosely connected implicit myths. It is often the therapist who puts these implicit myths together. The family's explanations of its problems is usually presented as an implicit family myth. When therapists rearrange these implicit myths according to their own frame of reference — one which is hopefully more conducive to change — they substitute a therapeutic myth for the dysfunctional myth.

Sharing the therapeutic myth, or part of it, with the family may be a difficult task, because it may differ considerably from the family's myth concerning the origin of the presenting problems. Therapists should only do this when they believe they know the family culture well and have a good working alliance with the family. In order to get the therapeutic myth accepted by the family, the therapists must speak the family's language, using the family's own images, metaphors and symbols.

When the family resists the therapists' direct explanation a more subtle approach is required. We are reminded here of van Baaren's remarks about the priests changing the content of a myth which is no longer in accordance with the political situation. Each time they recited the myth, they made small unobtrusive changes, until the text was wholly adapted to the new situation (van Baaren, 1972). Perhaps family therapists introducing changes in existing family myths do not need to be as careful and unobtrusive as the priests whose heads were at stake. Still, this narrative strategy — to borrow an expression from the psychoanalyst, Schafer (1983) — can better be seen as evolving over time than as being a one story affair.

Although the treatment described here eventually produced positive results, it also showed the adverse effects of a too direct attack upon the dominating family myth. After two conflicting family myths were elaborated, the therapeutic myth confronted the dominant myth, which legitimized the position of the stepmother. Probably because of this confrontation, the stepmother was depressed for three months and the family members decided to stop family therapy. Taking the course of direct confrontation instead of making small unobtrusive changes was, on the one hand, related to the obvious existence of two conflicting myths, but on the other hand, to the fact that the therapeutic team felt pressured to provide a breakthrough. Had the team realized this, the therapist would probably have protected the stepmother by positive reframing and by utilizing the fact that the children also had deep respect for her. The challenge for the children might then have been to show her that it was indeed possible in their family to both honor and respect Mama and to commemorate their beloved Mother.

3. Connecting Interventions on Both the Ideational and Material Plane of Family Culture

As mentioned before, our first therapeutic interventions are usually directed at the ideational plane of family culture. We believe, however, that in this case the value of the above presented alternative intervention would have been greatly enhanced by an additional intervention at the material level. The therapists could have suggested a ritual to honor Mama as well as a ritual commemorating Mother. The contents of these rituals could then have been developed together with the children. This would have given the children the challenge to acknowledge Mama's place in the family, while offering Mama the opportunity to acknowledge the fact that her sister was the children's Mother (and, implicitly, to acknowledge her contributions to the family and to build on them, instead of fighting them).

4. The Truth of Myths

Myths are true accounts for those who believe in them, but they are seen as distortions of reality by those who believe in something else. Therapists often do not see the families' narratives about the origin of their problems as completely correct. They believe more in the truth of their own narrative accounts. If the treatment, based upon their myth is successful, they will continue to believe in it (while it might have worked because of completely different reasons). Often, however, therapists feel compelled to revise their myths. With regard to the case example offered here, we would now develop a rather different therapeutic myth than the one which guided our interventions at the time. Moreover, other colleagues — e.g., those belonging to other schools — may have widely different views and would construct different narratives about the origin and continuation of the problems. Perhaps more than others, strategic family therapists believe in those myths which best promise change, but they also realize that the myths they come up with are usually not guaranteed to live very long.

REFERENCES

Anderson, S.A. & Bagarozzi, D.A. (1983). The use of family myths as an aid to strategic therapy. *Journal of Family Therapy, 5,* 145-154.

Bagarozzi, D.A. & Anderson, S.A. (1982). The evolution of family mythological systems: Considerations for meaning, clinical assessment, and treatment. *Journal of Psychoanalytic Anthropology, 5,* 71-90.

Bossard, J.H.S. & Boll, E.S. (1950). *Ritual in family living.* Philadelphia: University of Pennsylvania Press.

Byng-Hall, J. (1973). Family myths used as defence in conjoint family therapy. *British Journal of Medical Psychology, 46,* 239-250.

Cohen, P.S. (1969). Theories of myth. *Man,* N.S. IV, 337-353.

De Langhe, R. (1958). In S.H. Hooke (Ed.), *Myth, ritual, and kinship.* Oxford.

De Tempe, J. (1987). Grief therapy from an anthropological point of view. In O. van der Hart (Ed.), *Coping with loss: The therapeutic use of leave-taking rituals.* New York: Irvington.

Douglas, M. (1966). *Purity and danger.* New York: Praeger.

Drever, J.V. (1965). *A dictionary of psychology.* Middlesex: Penguin Books.

Dundes, A. (1984). Introduction. In A. Dundes (Ed.), *Sacred narrative.* Berkeley: University of California Press.

Durkheim, E. (1915). *The elementary forms of the religious life.* London: George Allen & Unwin.

Ferreira, A.J. (1963). Family myth and homeostasis. *Archives of General Psychiatry, 9,* 457-463.

Fontenrose, J. (1959). *Python: A study of Delphi myth and its origins.* Berkeley: University of California Press.

Frank, J. (1973). *Persuasion and healing: A comparative study of psychotherapy*. Baltimore: Johns Hopkins University Press.

Gaster, T.H. (1954). Myth and story. *Numen, 1*, 184-212.

Geertz, C. (1959). Ritual and change: A Javaneese example. *American Anthropologist, 61*, 991-1012.

Haley, J. (1973). *Uncommon therapy*. New York: W.W. Norton & Co.

Hoffman, L. (1980). The family life cycle and discontinuous change. In E. Carter & M. McGoldrick (Eds.), *The family life cycle: A framework for family therapy*. New York: Gardner Press.

Honko, L. (1972). The problem of defining myth. In H. Biezais (Ed.), *The myth of the state*. Stockholm: Scripta Instituti Donneriani Aboensis.

Janet, P. (1929). *L'Evolution psychologie de la personnalite*. Paris: A. Chahine.

Janet, P. (1935). Realisation et interpretation. *Annales Medico-Psychologiques, 93*, 329-366.

Kirk, G.S. (1970). *Myth: Its meaning and functions in ancient and other cultures*. Cambridge: Cambridge University Press.

Kirk, G.S. (1972). On defining myth. *Phronesis: A Journal for Ancient Philosophy, suppl. vol. 1*, 61-69.

Kluckholn, C. (1942). Myths and rituals: A general theory. *Harvard Theological Review, 35*, 45-79.

Kobak, R.R. & Waters, D.B. (1984). Family therapy as a rite of passage: Play's the thing. *Family Process, 23*, 89-100.

Laird, J. (1984). Sorcerers, shamans, and social workers: The use of ritual in social work practice. *Social Work, 29*, 123-129.

Lange, A. & van der Hart, O. (1983). *Directive family therapy*. New York: Brunner/Mazel.

Leach, E.R. (1954). *Political systems of Highland Birma*. London: University of London.

Levi-Strauss, C. (1963). The effectiveness of symbols. In C. Levi-Strauss (Ed.), *Structural Anthropology*. New York: Basic Books.

Malinowski, B. (1926). *Myth in primitive psychology*. London.

Minuchin, S. & Fishman, H.C. (1981). *Family therapy techniques*. Cambridge: Harvard University Press.

Moore, S.F. & Myerhoff, B.G. (1977). Introduction; secular ritual: forms and meanings. In S.F. Moore & B.G. Myerhoff (Eds.), *Secular ritual*. Assen: van Gorcum.

Munn, N. (1973). Symbolism in a ritual context: Aspects of symbolic action. In J.J. Honigmann (Ed.), *Handbook of social and cultural anthropology*. Chicago: Rand McNally & Co.

Murphy, R.F. (1971). *The dialectics of social life*. New York: Basic Books.

Papp, P. (1983). *The process of change*. New York: Guilford Press.

Pillari, V. (1986). *Pathways to family myths*. New York: Brunner/Mazel.

Sargent, G.A. (1987). A burial at sea. In O. van der Hart (Ed.) *Coping with loss: The therapeutic use of leave-taking rituals*. New York: Irvington.

Schafer, R. (1983). *The analytic attitude*. London: Hogarth.

Seltzer, W.J. & Seltzer, M.R. (1983). Material, myth and magic: A cultural approach to family therapy. *Family Process, 22*, 3-14.

Selvini Palazzoli, M. (1974). *Self Starvation: From the intrapsychic to the trans-personal approach to anorexia nervosa*. London: Chaucer.

Selvini Palazzoli, M., Boscolo, L., Cecchin, G.F. & Prata, G. (1974). The treatment of children through brief treatment of their parents. *Family Process, 16*, 429-442.

Selvini Palazzoli, M., Boscolo, L., Cecchin, G.F. & Prata, G. (1977). Family rituals: A powerful tool in family therapy. *Family Process, 16*, 445-454.

Siggins, L.D. (1983). Psychoanalysis and ritual. *Psychiatry, 46*, 2-15.

Skorupski, J. (1976). *Symbol and theory: A philosophical study of religion*. Cambridge: Cambridge University Press.

Stierlin, H. (1973). Group fantasies and family myths—some theoretical and practical aspects. *Family Process, 12*, 111-125.

Tennekes, J. (1979). *Cultuur als experiment*. Amsterdam: Vrije Universiteit.

Tennekes, J. (1982). *Symbolen en hun boodschap: Een inleiding in de symbolische anthropologie*. Assen: van Gorcum.

Ter Horst, V. (1977). *Het herstel van het gewone leven*. Kampen: Kok.

Turner, V.W. (1967). *The forest of symbols: Aspects of Ndembu ritual*. Ithaca: Cornell University Press.

Turner, V.W. (1977). Variations on a theme of liminality. In S.F. Moore & B.G. Myerhoff (Eds.), *Secular ritual*. Assen: van Gorcum.

Turner, V.W. (1978). Encounter with Freud: The making of a comparative symbologist. In G.D. Spindler (Ed.), *The making of a psychological anthropology*. Berkeley: University of California Press.

van Barren, T.P. (1972). The flexibility of myth. *Studies in the History of Religion, 22*, 199-206.

van der Hart, O. (1980). Problematische gezinssituaties. *Maanblad Geestelijke Volksgezondheid, 35*, 764-786.

van der Hart, O. (1983). *Rituals in psychotherapy: Transition and continuity*. New York: Irvington Publishers.

van der Hart, O. (1988a). Symbols in leave-taking rituals. In O. van der Hart (Ed.), *Coping with loss: The therapeutic use of leavetaking rituals*. New York: Irvington.

van der Hart, O. (1988b). Myths and rituals: Their use in psychotherapy. In O. van der Hart (Ed.), *Coping with loss: The therapeutic use of leave-taking rituals*. New York: Irvington.

Waardenburg, J. (1980). Symbolic aspects of myth. In A.M. Olson (Ed.), *Myth, symbol and reality*. Notre Dame: University of Notre Dame Press.

Mythmaking in the Land of Imperfect Specialness: Lions, Laundry Baskets and Cognitive Deficits

Janine Roberts

SUMMARY. Family myths are both homeostatic and morphogenic and they contain within them (as does symptomatic behavior) many of the necessary components for change. In this case report, the therapy process is described as primarily a place to see family mythology in development where plots can shift, endings can be changed and new characters introduced. Four central myths were explored with this family of mother, father and two young children by juxtaposing, rewriting and shifting the meaning of various family rituals, symbols and stories. Techniques that clinicians can use to work with the evolution of family myths are highlighted such as puppet shows, bringing in symbols, gift giving, telling of open ended fables and termination rituals.

Myths bring the unknown into relation with the known.

Cecile M. Bowra

Janine Roberts, EdD, is Director, Family Therapy Specialty Area School, Consulting & Counseling Psychology Program, 460 Hills South, University of Massachusetts, Amherst, MA 01003.

The author would like to extend special thanks to her generative partner in clinical practice, Dr. Richard (Dick) Whiting; and to this very creative family. Without them, none of this would have been possible. The author particularly appreciated the willingness of the clients to read the manuscript and allow her to incorporate their comments within it. The editing of Stephen A. Anderson and Dennis A. Bagarozzi as well as the anonymous reviewers was also very helpful.

WORKING DEFINITION OF MYTH
IN FAMILY THERAPY

When trying to answer the question "What is myth?" St. Augustine wrote in his *Confessions*, "I know very well what it is, provided that nobody asks me; but if I am asked and try to explain, I am baffled" (as quoted in Ruthven, 1976, p. 1). As family therapists have tried to explain myth, difficulties have arisen because a narrow homeostatic view of its functions has traditionally been applied. Ferreira's (1963) definition is commonly used as a starting place to articulate the place of mythology in families. Myths are:

> a series of fairly well-integrated beliefs shared by all family members concerning each other and their mutual position in family life, beliefs that go unchallenged by everyone involved in spite of the reality distortions which they may conspicuously imply. (p. 457)
> The struggle to maintain the myth is a struggle to maintain the relationship — a relationship that is obviously experienced as vital and, for which, it seems, the child may have no choice in reality, while the parents have no choice in fantasy. (p. 462)

The family therapy field has found it difficult to look at myths from a both/and perspective as is reflected in the most recent book on myth, *Pathways to Family Myths* (1986) by Vimela Pillari. While she gives lip service to the more positive aspects of myth, she concludes after her four detailed case studies that "Family myths protect the family from facing reality as it is and binds (sic) anxiety. They also function as a social facade and as a family's defense mechanism" (p. 171). Her analyses of the four families (done through extensive interviews with one elder of each family) focus on the negative and homeostatic side of myth, rather than the way myths also create meaning, cohesion and identity.

As noted by Feinstein (1979), part of the problem may be that "The word myth is tainted by its vernacular usage, where it refers to a falsehood" (p. 202). The field of anthropology had to move beyond the clichés of the Enlightenment and of Positivism that "'myth' meant anything that was opposed to reality" (Eliade, 1960, p. 23). Family therapy also needs to make this shift.

There is another problem with the traditional definition of myth by Ferreira. As Ruthven points out in the critical idiom book he wrote entitled *Myths* (1976), no one experiences "myth" per se, but only their cognitive interpretation and perception of a myth. The fact that the observer can only describe how they *perceive* a myth (since it exists only in the mind), needs to be operationalized in how myth is worked with in family therapy. What the therapist describes as myth may not be perceived by the family at all as myth, but may be seen as "reality." Ferreira's definition does not acknowledge the therapist as an observing system who gives the name myth to certain views of the family.

In recent years, other authors have tried to broaden Ferreira's original definition to highlight how myth can serve adaptive functions (Anderson & Bagarozzi, 1983); carry family history in a blend of both fact and fantasy (Steinglass, 1978) and how complex role images are contained within them (Byng-Hall, 1973). Cronen, Pearce and Tomm (1985) have also extended the definition of family myth beyond describing roles and family relationships to include higher order general conceptions of how society works (i.e., "the world is an unsafe place").

I have been particularly influenced by the position taken by Anderson and Bagarozzi (1983) where they go outside of the field of family therapy (particularly to anthropology) to look at how myth has been defined. This leads them to examine myth as a type of discourse (p. 148). In fact, as Keeney (1983) noted, "The stories people live as well as their stories about those stories are all that a therapist has to work with. In this sense, therapy is a conversation, an exchange of stories" (p. 195). Anderson and Bagarozzi describe the process of working with myths in therapy as one of helping the family rewrite its own script using the various rituals, symbols and metaphors that the family and therapist co-evolve. Ritual is seen as bringing action into the therapy process as they enact myths in both spoken and acted form. They emphasize the importance of working with symbols as a way to share implicit associations and themes that cannot be articulated in words. Also, as Turner has described

(1967), symbols have multi-vocality. Thus, they can carry multiple meanings as well as hold disparate meanings at the same time. A net for example can be seen as a symbol of safety, or as one of entrapment.

In this case report, *mythmaking* in families is seen as an evolutionary process which serves both homeostatic and morphogenic functions, where roles, self-images, shared historical experience and views of the world outside their family are all defined. Ways to examine mythmaking include the various symbols, stories and rituals which the family holds. Mythmaking contains within it connections to forces beyond the family as it joins with shared cultural symbols, images, and the process of creating stories throughout the history of all people. As Bateson (1979) noted, "A story is a little knot or complex of that species of connectedness which we call relevance . . . (and there) is connection between people in that all think in terms of stories" (p. 13).

Finally, it is important to qualify this definition of myth by noting that whoever gives the myth name (the observer), always influences it. As Freilich (1975) wrote, "Every myth analyst is also a myth maker" (p 217).

CASE REPORT: LIONS, LAUNDRY BASKETS AND COGNITIVE DEFICITS

Brief Description of Family

A professional couple in their late thirties came in asking for help both around entrenched patterns that had been a part of their seventeen year marriage, as well as help in parenting their two young sons, Abel (age 6) and Xavier (age 3). The family's genogram is reproduced in Figure 1.

Developmentally, this family was just leaving behind six years of very intensive care of infants and toddlers. As they moved into the life cycle phase of parenting young children, it seemed that they were stopping to look at and consolidate their family identity. As the parents (especially the mother) both moved back to working full time, there needed to be some readjustment of caretaking in the

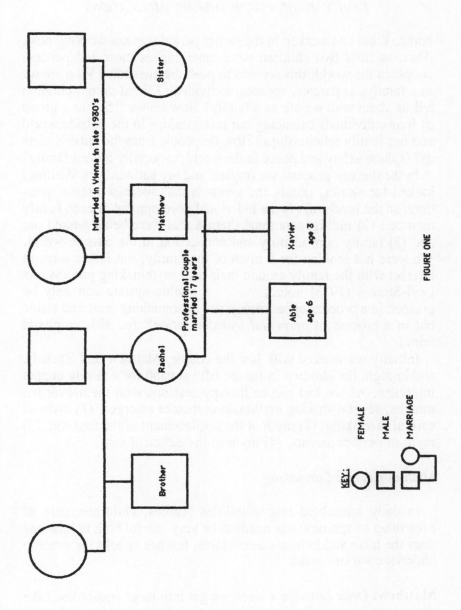

FIGURE ONE

KEY:

○ FEMALE

□ MALE

□—○ MARRIAGE

85

home. What had worked in the earlier period was not working now. Also, as their two children were emerging as more independent people in the world, this seemed to push the questions: Who are we as a family, as parents, spouses, individuals? What do our children tell us about who we are as a family? How do we "fit" as a group of four individuals balancing our relationships in the outside world and our family relationships? How do people from the outside view us? Is there safety and peace in the world, especially for our family?

In the therapy process, we (myself and my partner Dick Whiting) looked for stories, rituals and symbols that addressed these questions on the levels of: (1) the individual development of each family member; (2) multigenerational themes that were being passed on; and (3) family core identity and connection to the outside world. We were not looking for *a* myth of the family, but rather ways to interact with the family around their own mythmaking process. As Levi-Strauss (1973) noted, ". . . a mythic system can only be grasped in a *process of becoming*; not as something inert and stable but in a process of *perpetual transformation*" (p. 354, emphasis mine).

Initially we worked with just the couple (Matthew and Rachel), and brought the children in for the fifth session for a family puppet interview. As we had eleven therapy sessions with them over ten months, several striking mythmaking themes emerged: (1) myth of careful caretaking, (2) myth of the displacement of the first son, (3) myth of perfect parents, (4) myth of the deficient son.

Myth of Careful Caretaking

In daily household responsibilities (chores, childcare, care of each other as spouses) one needs to be very careful both in how one does the tasks and in how one explains, teaches or asks the other to undertake various tasks.

Matthew: Once or twice a week we get into these squabbles. Like around the laundry. Rachel will wash the clothes and leave them in the dryer for days. I won't let her do my shirts and pants because they get too wrinkled. The laundry never gets folded and put away.

Rachel: He's always trying to teach me how to do things. I feel like I'm giving up a sense of autonomy of being able to do it my way. Either I defend myself or I give in.

For Matthew, the issue connected to this myth was "am I being taken care of?" Things being organized and clean around the house made him feel that he was cared for. For Rachel the issue connected to this myth was "is my autonomy being taken away?" She liked a looser, more flexible schedule by which to do housework and also was not as particular as Matthew about the way things needed to be done. She felt overly criticized by him.

When the couple was first married and in their many years together without children, they had shared quite equally the cooking, cleaning, shopping, etc. After the birth of the second son, there seemed to be a shift where the husband took on more of the daily concerns about household chores being done as well as taking on more tasks than he had before. This meant a lot to Rachel and in fact, she felt very cared for by this change. This necessary shift when they had two very young children at home and Rachel was doing more of the childcare hadn't seemed to successfully shift again as the children got older and needed less intensive attention. Rather, Matthew seemed to be withdrawing from doing as much around the house, while complaining more about what Rachel was not doing. Further, their two very different ways of doing tasks clashed and they were having a hard time organizing the household in a way that respected their two styles. Both parents worked quite demanding jobs.

A *ritual* that had evolved in their daily family life (Wolin & Bennett, 1984) that enacted this myth was how, where and when to do the laundry. The more haphazardly Rachel did the clothes, the more organized Matthew wanted the wash routine. The more Matthew criticized Rachel's way of washing and drying and folding clothes, the more laid back she became about it all. Clothes and laundry baskets became *symbols* in the therapy for this myth — clean clothes, dirty clothes, folded clothes, unfolded, socks matched and unmatched, pajamas sized and put away, clothes in the dryer, on top of the dryer, in the living room. Dick and I wondered when we might have a hand at doing the clothes.

An essential *story* that emerged in the eighth session that was connected to the theme of caretaking was the near drowning of their second son some eleven months earlier. The family had been in Georgia on vacation and Matthew was to be watching Xavier (age 3) at the pool while Rachel was swimming. Rachel was doing laps and emerged, looking for Xavier. She asked Matthew, who was reading near the pool, "Where is Xavier?" They found him face down in the water. Healing needed to be done about this time of not careful caretaking. Would they have been able to go on if they had lost him? Would the parents still be able to care for each other? What was most important in terms of their caretaking responsibilities? Did they really have "control" over their lives?

Work done on this area in therapy. We began by looking at the strengths of both of their organizational styles. Matthew brought focus and energy to tasks, Rachel brought a spontaneity which highlighted that other priorities are more important in life than household responsibilities. We first asked them to do a variation of the Selvini-Palazzoli et al. (1978) odd days, even days ritual: They were to alternate weeks of doing the chores first in Rachel's style and then in Matthew's. During this time they were to observe the impact of each of these styles on three sets of relationships: parents and children; parents as spouses and parents as parents. With feedback from this experiment, we worked with them to find a type of schedule that utilized both of their strengths and that they could both commit to, rather than one indirectly trying to get the other to follow his/her preferred style of doing things. They came up with a prioritized flexible schedule of things to be done within broad time frames with the most important things listed first. We also looked extensively at the household responsibilities as a metaphor for the care each felt from the other. We discussed what signals they had from the other when they were feeling harried and needed more care, what other kinds of care they received from each other, and ways to acknowledge to the other when they experienced the care.

Tasks were delineated more clearly. They came up with job definitions of household responsibilities that they could agree on. When one person was doing something, the other was to back off from criticizing how the other did it. They were to trust that they would respect the agreed upon job description.

We played a lot with the laundry. When the unfolded laundry was laying around, we encouraged them to use it in dress up with the kids when they wanted to break a tense interaction. For instance, Xavier was wrapped up in some of it by the parents when he was having a temper tantrum, and he emerged laughing with some underpants on his head. They also got the kids to help them fold the laundry up. A basket was purchased just to put washed socks in to let the kids find matching ones rather than the parents sorting them. A game was made out of pajamas not fitting when they were in the wrong child's drawer.

Finally, there was a retelling of the near drowning story with us as witnesses. This was a story that had not been shared with their own parents who were in the vacation house, and it was a story that Rachel in particular felt they had never fully discussed. They needed to talk through the horror of what might have happened and if they could have survived it. As Rachel said:

> The session where we talked about what happened with Xavier was powerful for me. I felt a real sense of being able to let go after that. I always felt like talking about it (the near drowning) made me not hold on to it so much. I have felt less concerned with it. Talking about it really helped.

A different set of rituals began to evolve around the myth where each spouse recognized the importance to the other of the meaning attached to caretaking.

II. Myth of the Displacement of the Firstborn Son

Abel acts out of control at times (hitting Xavier, not getting along with peers) because he has never gotten over the birth of his younger brother. We will never be able to make this up to him.

Father: Xavier is now almost three and Abel (age 6) has not gotten over his birth yet and is still having a lot of reaction.
Mother: The first two years after Xavier was born were very hard. Abel was first very angry at me, and then at Xavier.

The parents bent over backwards to prepare Abel for the birth of Xavier and felt in retrospect that perhaps they had talked about it too much and been too encouraging of Abel's negative feelings about his younger brother. The explanation that Abel was hurt by Xavier's birth seemed to make the parents more lenient of some of his behavior than they might otherwise have been.

The *ritual* in day to day family life where this myth was enacted was limit setting for Abel. When Rachel put limits on some of Abel's behavior, he would get very upset and ask her to still hug and kiss him even if he was supposed to be isolated in his room. Out of her ambivalence about the punishment, Rachel would go to him, trying to give him the message "it's your behavior at this time I don't like. I still like you."

Matthew disagreed with this message, feeling it only muddled the communication for kids. He felt it was O.K. not to like a child for awhile, that they could learn that part of the consequences of some types of behavior (such as hitting) is that a parent might not like them for a short period of time.

Two important *symbols* that evolved in the family created puppet show in the fifth session were Abel as the bad lion and Xavier as the good wolf. This puppet show also contained within it an essential *story*. Abel emerged through his lion puppet as the King of the Forest that everyone was trying to cajole into behaving better. The more other family members tried to find ways to connect with him, the more raucous his behavior became. (To begin the puppet show, the family was given a box of twenty different animal, people and fantasy puppets that were *not* distinguishable as any particular character [like Mickey Mouse]. They were each asked to choose one puppet that they liked and to give it a name and a voice and present it to the group. The family was then asked to create their own story [not a story they already knew like "Little Red Riding Hood"] with the puppets. See Irwin and Malloy [1975] for further instructions on family puppet interviews.)

"How to Save the Lion" (Mother's title)
"Try to Make Friends with the Lion" (Father's title)

Panther the Pirate (mother's puppet) and Henry the Rooster (father's puppet) are friends going for a walk in the woods. Wolfie (Xavier's puppet) and Beetle Eyes the Lion (Abel's puppet) attack them.

Rachel: Will you be a nice friendly wolf?
Xavier: Yes.
Rachel: Lion, will you be angry or . . . (Lion attacks the pirate.)
Matthew: (sitting over on the side) Lion, are you part of the show?
Xavier: I'm good. I'm good.
Abel: I'm good too. (Abel drops his lion puppet over the edge of the sofa which is the puppet stage and starts climbing over the sofa to get it.)
Rachel: Abel, why don't you go around. (Abel continues to climb over.)
Xavier: I'm good. Where's the chicken? (meaning dad's rooster puppet).
Matthew: You're a good wolf now. Do you want to be our friend and go for a walk in the woods with us?
Xavier: Yes.
Matthew: What about your friend Lion?
Xavier: O.K. He can come as long as he is good. I'll make him good.
Rachel: How will you make him be good?
Xavier: I have magic (makes swirling motions). The wolf has magic. (Lion attacks the wolf.)
Rachel: (putting her arm around Xavier) I have to protect Wolfie.
Matthew: Oh Lion, why are you being such an angry lion?
Abel: Someone stole my eggs (hits the rooster puppet).
Rachel: I stole the eggs, and put them on the boat.
Matthew: Why did you steal the eggs, Pirate?
Rachel: I wanted Lion to be my friend, to come and find me on my boat. Guess what I have on my boat. A swimming pool, running track, swing set. Will you come on my boat? (to Abel).
Abel: Does it have a big pool?
Matthew: What about Wolfie and Chicken (rooster), are they invited too? (Abel takes his puppet off and is grabbing the other puppets.)

Matthew: If you are angry at Wolfie and Pirate why are you angry at us? (Abel throws his lion puppet overboard onto the floor on the other side of the puppet theatre [the sofa]. Then he climbs over the sofa again.)
Xavier: Now he won't fight over you two guys.
Rachel: We better rescue the lion.
Abel: Mommy, pull me up. (Rachel pulls Abel and the lion puppet back aboard.)
Rachel: Oh boy, we saved the lion.
(Abel throws the puppet overboard again as well as himself.)
Matthew: Let's figure out how lion will get to be friends with us.
Abel: I'm not going to be friends.
Xavier: (standing up proudly) Well, I'm good.
Rachel: Lion, will you be my friend? (No response from Abel.)
Xavier: I'll be your friend.
Rachel: What shall we do to save Lion?
Xavier: What shall we do to save Lion?
Matthew: Do you want us to rescue you, Lion? (Abel continues to play off by himself on the other side of the room.)
Xavier: I'm good, I'm good (holding his wolf puppet up high in the air).

Work done in this area in therapy. Immediately after the puppet show, we asked the family to compare the story of the show to how things go at home. The parents talked about ways they bent over backwards to try to help Abel and how the show reflected that Abel had never forgiven Rachel for having Xavier. As Matthew said, "You took the eggs away." Xavier didn't like the lion puppet because "he was grabbing at this one and this one and this one." Abel didn't like Wolfie "because he was mean."

We asked the parents to take home the videotape of the puppet show, to look at it and discuss ways they could set limits for Abel's behavior other than trying to talk him into cooperating more and cajoling him with special favors. We also talked about ways to chart his behaviors to reward him when he was acting appropriately. The parents were very struck by the good character/bad character dichotomy of the puppet show. At home, they worked hard to catch

Abel in his many competencies and acknowledge these more, as well as to see the negative aspects of some of Xavier's behavior. They also decided to intervene earlier with Abel, putting limits on his actions before they got out of control.

III. Myth of Perfect Parents

We must be better parents than our parents because no matter how perfect you are, and how overvigilant, terrible things can happen (like the Holocaust).

Father: Rachel tries to do things for the kids that she feels were not done for her. Projects with them, reading to them, participating much more actively. Things she didn't get.
Mother: That (family history of losses in the Holocaust) had a lot to do with my bringing up. Proprietary, doing the right thing, behaving properly, being polite. . . . Once I reached adolescence my need to flounder around was very threatening to my parents. In my parents' view, you get a profession, get settled. Safety.

For Rachel, this myth was played out in the arena of wanting to be a more involved parent than either of her parents. She felt her mother did not do many active things with her and that her father was pretty much on the periphery of the family. For Matthew, the message from his family of origin was no matter how perfect you are, terrible things can happen. Therefore, it was necessary to work very hard to protect things of importance to you — to be overvigilant. As a child, Matthew felt this was embodied for him in an important rule not to make waves, to try somehow to make up to his parents for their terrible losses. "Don't make it worse by misbehaving." This message was carried through to the current generation by Matthew's statement, "I owe my parents having perfect grandchildren."

A *ritual* in day to day life where this myth was enacted was while the parents were involved in such a marvelous range of activities with the children (swimming, biking, skiing, nature walks, gardening, chess, stories), they watched each other and themselves very intently as parents. They were quite self-critical and did not give themselves much leeway as parents.

A *symbol* that emerged in therapy (when we asked them to think of what they had in their house that was imperfectly special) was a box that was hand made by the wife with no nails or screws, but that had never been finished with the cabinet doors on the front. Yet the box had its own beauty in the integrity of the design, the wood and its functionality even without the doors.

Key *stories* emerged for each of the parents. Rachel's went as follows:

> I was the second child. My brother was much more connected with my mother emotionally. I was more emotionally connected with my father. I was basically a good kid. I didn't ask for much. My mom tells me what a good kid I was. My response was "You didn't give me any attention."

Matthew's story was:

> My parents were married in Vienna in the late 1930s. Not a legal or good thing to be doing—to have a Jewish wedding. So they had a very small wedding. In the wedding picture, my parents look very happy; the rest of the wedding party looks very grim. An aunt in that picture committed suicide, other relatives shown there died in the camps, or escaped to Palestine not to be seen for twenty years. That picture frames that experience in many ways.

Work done in this area in therapy. We asked the couple to put the imperfectly special box out on the kitchen table. (This was a place highlighted by the wife as where she felt connection in the family. We had been doing some work in sessions around gender and where she "fit" in a family where there were three males and one female.) Matthew volunteered to rescue the box from obscurity in the basement. We wanted it out in a central place as a symbol of imperfect specialness and we also asked Matthew to put in the box any particular things over the next few weeks that symbolized for him times when he felt particularly joined to Rachel.

On their own, the parents picked up a copy of *Dr. Gardner's*

Stories about the Real World (1976). They read these stories about socially appropriate behavior to the two children together and separately. They had their effect on both the children and the storytellers (the parents). As Rachel said, "(In reading those stories) I realized it was important for me to be able to set limits with him (Abel). I moved out of trying to make him do something—a power struggle—to trying to teach him something that was important for me to learn how to do."

Other key events occurred over one weekend when friends came to stay with Rachel and Matthew who had a child near Abel's age.[1] Rachel particularly used them as a sounding board to ask them what they observed about her parenting. They told her that they saw her as ambivalent about setting limits for Abel and that he seemed aware of it. As the father said, "Punishments are not supposed to be pleasant for kids." This pushed Rachel to think about how she tried to protect Abel from feeling hurt by any limit setting.

In another session, we told the couple an unfinished fable:

Janine: (after returning from an intersession discussion with Dick) We have a fable. (Matthew and Rachel laugh.)
Matthew: We thought you might have done that. (Both sit back.)
Janine: And it is about a King and Queen who live in a Land of Imperfect Specialness. (Rachel and Matthew look at each other and smile.) They are a King and Queen who are very much loved by their people because they pay much attention to personal relationships of people, quality of life and talk a lot with the people about what they are thinking and feeling. It is very much appreciated by the people especially since this is a kingdom which lived through a terrible disaster. They are a small group of people who survived an earthquake and landslide. Many of their villages were destroyed. (Matthew looks down, more pensive. Rachel moves her head over to one side, carefully listening.)

As the King was doing more and more outside the castle, the Queen became more the keeper of day to day things in the castle — keeper of the anxieties of the castle. They held off having their own children until they felt like many things in the Kingdom were in place. So they waited for some time until they had their first princeling. (Rachel sits up with a small laugh.)

The princeling was very special to both of them because of the disaster that had befallen many of the villagers several generations before, because of their attention to people and also because they had waited and talked and thought for a long time how they would like the royal family to be. They wanted very much for their princeling to experience that specialness. They would take pictures of him (Matthew and Rachel look at each other and smile) and he would squirm and wonder what was this specialness they wanted him to experience. Over time, in some ways he got to know perhaps more specialness than he needed. And when the second princeling was about to come along, the King and Queen, especially the Queen, redoubled their efforts to let the first son know that he was continuing to be very special and he had a very unique place in this family.

They wanted people outside the castle and outside the Kingdom to experience the children in that way as well. But over time, the King and Queen began to realize that some of the specialness was turning out not to be special. It was getting to be something different than how they had imagined specialness and they began to make some changes in how they treated the first princeling and the second princeling, especially the Queen as the castle had become so much her domain.

And where the storytellers are right now (both sit up, laugh and move together) is the Queen in this Land of Imperfect Specialness — the Queen who in her own way wants to be very perfect and special — needs some support as she moves towards realizing the beauty of imperfect specialness and realizing this is something both of the princelings have. What the storytellers are wondering is how that support is going to happen. Is it through other people in the Kingdom supporting her in her changes as she comes to accept the imperfect specialness both in herself and of her princelings? Is it going to come from the King (they look at each other and smile) as he appreciates the changes she has been doing? Or it is going to come through making up fantasies or stories to tell to others in the Kingdom? We're not sure and we'd like to ask you to finish the fable. O.K.?

Rachel: O.K. We should finish the fable.

Matthew: O.K.

Rachel: You did a nice job of making up a fable.

Matthew: O.K. We'll take it . . .
Janine: We look forward to that.
Rachel: To the end of the fable?
Janine: Yes.
Rachel: O.K., in the land of imperfect specialness.

Finally, the story book *The Velveteen Rabbit* by Margery Williams was given to the family over the December holidays by the therapists as a way to share the theme of imperfect specialness with the whole family. (The rabbit is made of only velveteen, not velvet and so is snubbed by other animals in the nursery. He is discovered later on by the boy who lives in the nursery and is much loved by him, until one day the rabbit has to be thrown out because he is carrying scarlet fever germs. However, the rabbit has been loved so deeply that the magic Fairy of the nursery emerges from the rabbit's tear and makes him real, something that the Velveteen Rabbit had always wanted.)

IV. Myth of the Deficient Son

A cognitive problem has been passed down genetically on the father's side of the family to the oldest son.

Father: My older sister thought Abel had what her son Kerry (now 21) had and that she caught it too late. (Kerry had a difficult adolescence and made a serious suicide attempt and was hospitalized for several months.) An issue my sister came up with was that she and her son have difficulty with internal imaging. Say you ask a person to think of what their mother looks like. My sister and her son have a lot of difficulty doing that. I have some. She thinks this makes it difficult to have object constancy and interferes with the development of object relations. A month after Xavier was born, my sister was very concerned about Abel's reaction. She thought Abel had what Kerry had.

The parents had Abel observed by the school psychologist and had questions about whether to have him tested further or not. They were concerned about his ambidextrousness, and that at times he had coordination difficulties and emotional outbursts. They thought these might all be related to cognitive deficits.

Rituals in day to day life where this myth was enacted focused on trying to make up this possible deficit to the son. First, the parents excused various behaviors of Abel and were more lenient with him than they might have been. Second, they watched over him closely for what he couldn't do. The more they watched him, the more aware they all became of what he was having difficulty with, and the more anxious Abel became. For instance, they were concerned about his sports skills and Matthew would be encouraged to go out and do more sports practice with Abel even though this would not be his or his son's first choice of what they would want to do. Abel would then find himself doing activities where he was not able to show off his considerable competencies.

The velveteen rabbit was a *symbol* for something that was imperfectly special but was much loved. An important *story* in the therapy process was the saga of what Matthew's sister and son went through and the discovery of the cognitive deficit which freed them up from years of blame about who was at fault for the turmoil.

Work done in this area in therapy. We gave feedback to the parents on our own view of Abel's behavior when we saw him: that it seemed well within normal range of children that age and that he seemed particularly bright at ferreting out loopholes in any disciplinary actions. We also gave them the names of several people that had excellent reputations for further neurological testing and recommended to them that they follow this up if they thought it would be useful. We also discussed his teachers' and the school psychologist's observations. They were not recommending further testing at this time.

We asked if they had any written materials that they could get from either Matthew's sister or her therapist about the cognitive deficit problem so we could become more informed about it. (They had in fact called the therapist several years earlier to talk to her about Abel and at that time she was not concerned about Abel having an imaging problem.) We commented on how finding that problem had worked very well for Matthew's sister and her son in terms of getting them out of a cycle of blame they had been stuck in for some years, and wondered if Matthew and Rachel needed something like that or not. Finally, we discussed ways Abel would be treated differently by them if they did find he had a cognitive imaging problem. They felt they would be more patient, respond to him more quickly, work more specifically with him on certain skills. On the contrary, if they thought he didn't have a genetic problem, they thought they would be less lenient, and less ambivalent about limit setting. We then asked them to experiment with an odd days/even days ritual (Selvini-Palazzoli et al., 1978) where on odd days they would treat him as if he *did* have the deficit and they would observe both their behavior as well as Abel's. On even days, they were to treat him as if he *didn't* have the deficit and again observe their own behavior and his response to it. This seemed to have the effect of them incorporating more of all of the above behaviors as desirable parenting skills.

OUTCOME

How did each of these myths evolve through the therapy process? Dialogue is excerpted from the last session (except where noted), to capture the shifts. Parts of the termination ritual that we did with the family are also described where they brought in symbols of the therapy process to share and we gave them a small gift in appreciation for the gift of working with them in therapy. Everyone broke up with laughter when Matthew entered the last session with a basket of laundry. Symbols that Rachel brought included the imperfectly special box, and copies of *The Velveteen Rabbit* and *Dr. Gardner's Stories About the Real World*.

In the latter part of treatment, we had moved more to a reflecting team model (Anderson, 1987) where we had the couple watch our intersession discussions. In the last session, Dick came out from behind the mirror for the therapist's termination ritual (Imber-Black, Roberts, Whiting, in press), asking three question: What was most useful in treatment? Least useful? What advice would you give to other families with similar problems?

I. Myth of Careful Caretaking

Rachel: We haven't gotten into that battle at home (the housekeeping battle) in a long time.
Matthew: What's good for me to know is that Rachel has heard it (the importance of being careful with caretaking) — she doesn't have to do it all the time.

Matthew brought as a symbol of the therapy process a laundry basket of clean folded clothes with a dish towel on top (embroidered by Rachel when she was a girl) which said, "Iron on Tuesday." He purposely chose a basket with laundry from the whole family — "stuff that belongs to everybody." When asked how this basket was connected to the process of therapy he said:

> We spent an inordinate amount of time here discussing the laundry and it became symbolic of issues having to do with care, control, whether we agree to — how we do things together. Just how important is it? Joking around about it, put it in its proper place so to speak. . . . This is ridiculous coming in every week and talking about the laundry. (What helped in therapy) was the ability to look at it with a different perspective. Changing priorities. Commitment to each other instead of commitment to the laundry.

Each of the parent's positions had shifted. Matthew recognized that scheduling house cleaning was not going to be Rachel's first priority and he had to have a certain flex with that, but he appreciated Rachel's willingness to move to a position of acknowledging that certain things had to be done on a regular basis whether she spontaneously wanted to do them or not. Rachel recognized that structuring tasks helped to keep things organized and was more wiling to follow through on a regular basis.

About half way through therapy — mostly on the couple's initiative — Matthew stopped criticizing Rachel in front of the kids, and by the end of therapy Rachel felt that Matthew was less critical of her in private as well.

They had moved to a problem solution behavior of "we need to sit down and work this through together" rather than pointing the finger at each other of what had not been done. The symbolism of the household took on the meaning of collaborative care, not critical care.

II. Myth of the Displacement of the Firstborn Son

Rachel (6th session): A number of different changes have happened and we came to a number of different decisions. (Goes on to describe a reward system for Abel where he gets points for helpful behaviors and limits set on his hitting, teasing, etc.) . . . Both of us are really being consistent with him. There was an amazing turnaround. The incidents with Xavier were practically diminished.

There's a lot more nice playing together of the two boys. . . . Abel has responded to the structure and limits we've set for him and is into a very creative phase now. He's been able to try new things he couldn't try before like roller skating. He's been up in his room drawing and building. Two weeks ago he had a friend over. It's just a real difference of how he is relating to his friend — negotiating, talking, playing. As he feels better about himself, he plays with Xavier more.

Matthew (last session): More and more times the kids are able to play together now.
Rachel: I don't feel the same sense of worry that Abel will be off the wall, will hurt Xavier.

The puppet show session (fifth meeting) and subsequent visit from friends (where they gave feedback especially to Rachel on her parenting), seemed to be the turning point in the parents being clear with Abel that he had to adjust to being the older brother (and not the only child). From that time on, the parents gave more structure and limits and he responded well.

When discussing the meaning of the puppet show, Rachel said: He's never forgiven me for the fact I had Xavier.
Matthew: You took the eggs away.
Rachel: Abel was very impacted by losing the status of the only child. (I went on to ask Abel what he remembered about when

Xavier was born. In that discussion **Xavier** said): I ask my mom to kill my brother.

Janine: She's not going to do that.

Rachel: He has said that (kill Xavier) other times.

Janine: Does he sense you don't like to hear that? (Parents nod yes.) Does he get limits set on him for talking about Xavier that way?

Parents: No.

In the last session, Rachel described what was more helpful in the therapy process:

> There were a number of things I think were most helpful. The video with the kids. Doing the puppet show and then watching it with the kids. Realizing the categories of good and bad they were using. And your not freaking out that the kids were off the wall. That was important. That felt normalized in that kind of way. That was the beginning of normalizing things with Abel . . . (sixth session) What helped me from the puppet show is when you said, "Maybe you could rescue him (Lion, the King of the Forest) by limit setting."

Rachel (last session): In the puppet show they did here, it really hit home how Abel identified himself as the bad kid and Xavier the good kid. How they really split that. I think if they did the puppet show again it wouldn't come out like that—that's really changed.

III. Myth of Perfect Parents

Matthew: (in commenting on the parents' discussion of how to finish the fable) One of the things that came out of it was to just accept the imperfections as part of that which enhances things more.

Rachel: I really enjoyed the fairy tale that you told us and I found that very supportive. It gave the sense of acceptance—helped me accept where I was at more. I didn't have to be perfect—that was fine, that was O.K. It helped me trust more the process at that point with a renewed sense of being able to let my guard down. Accepted for who I was so I found it easier to be myself more.

The finishing of the fable captures the parents' work with the mythology of perfect parents. This was read to us in the seventh session by Rachel. (The beginning of the story as presented by the parents was a restatement of all the things that had gone so well in terms of the King and Queen's life: conceiving exactly when they wanted to, having jobs they liked, taking time from work when they wanted, etc. They also talked about how the Holocaust history and the near drowning of Xavier raised deep questions about how much control the King and Queen really had over this "perfect" life.)

Anxiety about the children being perfect remained with the older Prince while the younger Prince seemed immune from such pressures. He was allowed to grow up as he pleased and was enjoyed while the elder Prince was watched carefully and every behavior examined. While the elder Prince was always praised, the anxiety over what he was not doing was always transmitted to him.

In the quest for the Prince to fit into his parents' perfect life, he became less and less perfect. His parents, grandparents, cousins worried about him as if his behaviors were a precursor of even more difficulties later. They wanted the Prince to be happy and saw him become more and more unhappy. The Queen who was used to figuring things out decided the Prince needed more structure and needed to learn not to hurt others and to share for if he did not learn these skills, he would be lonely and have difficulties making friends. The Queen set out to accomplish this task. She learned she needed to appreciate his imperfections as something that makes him unique and special. While he is not always well behaved, he has a zest for life and is very creative. He may not stay within the lines but he creates much nicer pictures with his own artsy style.

She needs to set appropriate limits and not worry about his every step along the way. The King needs to learn that he does not need to control everything, particularly his older son. He also needs to let go of the image of the perfect child, the child who would please his parents, the child he was supposed to be. The end.

In the last therapy session after the couple shared their four symbols of the therapy process, I gave them each a T-shirt as a gift. Rachel's said on it "Celebrate imperfectly special mothers" and

Matthew's said, "Celebrate imperfectly special fathers." Our message to them was that we found them special with their everyday human imperfections. Upon getting the shirt Rachel said, "That's great. That's very nice. We'll be imperfect."
Matthew: Guarantee it.
Rachel: But special.

IV. Myth of the Deficient Son

Rachel: One of the things I was probably most upset about was what was happening with Abel and the whole notion of was there something the matter with Abel and I've decided that there is not and that he's O.K. Some skills he could be better at but there are some specific kinds of things he needs help with rather than the notion he's damaged in some genetic way.

   Part of my being able to set limits with him is because I wasn't compensating for something being the matter and so I was better able to set the limits.

   The parents decided not to go ahead with any further testing of Abel at this time. They felt that he responded very well to their changes in parenting and they also had concerns about him going through a labelling process that could hurt him in other ways. What was striking was how Matthew and Rachel were able to incorporate both sides of different parenting styles that they thought would be helpful to Abel if he was deficient (more structure, patience, responding to him more quickly when he was having difficulty) and if he was not deficient (clearer limits and less leniency regarding unacceptable behaviors).

MYTHWORKING TECHNIQUES

   This case demonstrates the use of open ended techniques which leave much space to co-create with families an understanding of mythological patterns. The *puppet show* allowed even very young children to contribute their discourse about how they saw the family. It also gave us a story to compare to daily life at home. In the comparisons, an elucidation of patterns of good child/bad child and parental ambivalence about limit setting emerged. Dick and I then asked the parents to take the video of the puppet show and look at other ways limit setting might have occurred within the context of that story. The parents watched the show both with the kids and without them. This gave them a chance to look at their own interactions with a little distance (on tape). They learned much from their children's version of their family and ultimately the story line of the puppet show shifted to two children that are both naughty and good.

Storytelling was a technique in which meaning could spiral back and forth between families of origin and this family, the therapy team and the two generations within the nuclear family. We got started on storytelling by my talking with Rachel and Matthew about how my daughter was so intrigued by stories about my early life. I used her interest to tell her stories with content about the issues she was currently struggling with (nightmares, having mixed feelings at the same time, and large group time at school). I encouraged Matthew, as he talked about the ways he saw Abel acting towards him as he acted towards his father (e.g., procrastination as quiet rebellion), to tell Abel stories about times he did similar things to his own father. Storytelling in this kind of situation can work on several levels. One, it validates for the child that it is O.K. to have the kinds of thoughts and feelings they might be experiencing. It also gives both the parent and child empathy for each other's position. For instance, as the parent talks about how he procrastinated, that creates a connection to what is currently happening with the child's delaying tactics. After Matthew began telling Abel some of these stories, Rachel bought Gardner's book of stories to read to children. In the session in which she talked about the benefit of reading these stories to their two kids she said, "But I can't make up stories." However, in the next session, she in fact came in with an elaborate end of a story to our unfinished fable and described two stories she had made up for her children. "I told Xavier a story the other day also. I've been into storytelling. Xavier gets his in the form of monster and boy stories. He was having a hard time at school with a kid that didn't want to play with him. So I told him a story about a boy with a monster that didn't want to play with him. He wanted to play with another friend. Xavier liked that story."

By telling the open ended fable, by having them make up their own story line in the puppet show, by encouraging them to connect with their children with stories about themselves as children, we encouraged an open ended search for different tales, endings, variations. As Keim, Lentine, Keim and Madanes have noted (1987),

> If a therapist must have a theory of personality to work with, then the most helpful one would be that of identity as a mental, abridged anthology of stories, any one of which can be replaced by a story from the total collection. Therapy thus involves re-editing the abridged edition of one's perceptions of the present and past. A change in these perceptions is a change in the personality, and a change of shared perceptions is a change in the relationship. (p. 16-17)

Symbols that emerged from the family (the laundry), ones we asked them to specifically name (the imperfectly special box) and ones the therapists introduced (*The Velveteen Rabbit*) were worked with throughout the therapy process. These symbols gave access to multiple levels of meaning as well as offered concrete ways to build connections between work done in sessions and day to day life at home. For instance, in the last session when I presented the couple with their T-shirts, we talked about ways these T-shirts could be used at home to mark their imperfect specialness: to put them on each other, to lay them out to remind themselves, to put them on top of the laundry basket, etc. Hopefully those shirts will carry the message for the family as therapy ended of how special the therapists thought the parents were.

Cross-hatching of meaning between the symbols was fascinating in the therapy process. For instance, the laundry basket shifted from the symbol of differences about how to housekeep to "this housekeeping stuff is not so significant." Rachel brought in the box of imperfect specialness at the end as "symbolic of recognizing I can't make Matthew do things he doesn't want to do. Matthew shows his caring in other kinds of ways. I need to accept those ways."

Janine: How did this box come to be symbolic of that?
Rachel: Because this was the box he refused to put things in and also the box of my imperfections.
Rachel: *The Velveteen Rabbit* was brought in not only because of

its theme of imperfectly being special, but because you gave it to us. It was a nice connection. That was special.

Symbols can take on a density of meaning beyond what words can do, provide concrete links to work being done outside of therapy, and provide an anchor point around which to discuss mixed and diffuse feelings.

Finally, the *termination ritual* as described in this case provides ways to highlight what the family has learned, mark their resources and to end the therapy more as equals. The family is asked to go meta to the process and comment on where it did and didn't work. Giftgiving from the therapists equalizes somewhat the imbalance of all of the gifts the family has given of sharing their life. If therapy is thought about in relation to Van Gennep's (1960) three stage process of ritual (separation, transitional and reintegration), the termination ritual works to reintegrate the family back to their day to day life. The team comes out from behind the one way mirror, marking "we are out of therapy." The symbols shared offer a place to summarize what happened in treatment and to concretely link the meaning of them to their life that will go on after therapy. Gifts can highlight family strengths.

Working with techniques such as symbols, rituals, storytelling and use of the arts has important implications for training clinicians. It can be crucial for them to examine the process of mythmaking in their own families of origin as a way to practice these techniques, gain other ideas of how they might be used with families, and have empathy for how they work. If they can be intrigued by how these processes worked in their own families, they will want to tap it in others.

FOLLOW-UP

After I wrote this article, I gave it to the parents to read and comment upon. We then met for several hours in their home. Their feedback helped me to clarify and sharpen a number of points which I incorporated right into the manuscript. The parents also appreciated how the paper pulled together for them in one place the various issues they had addressed. They felt like the process of reading about themselves helped them to consolidate their understanding of some patterns as well as see some new connections. For instance, Rachel commented, "I hadn't really connected those two points (Matthew's criticisms of her caretaking and when Matthew did not take care when Xavier almost drowned) until I read this paper. I thought, 'How dare you criticize my caretaking when you weren't being careful when it really mattered' (the near drowning)." As I have co-authored other case reports with families (Roberts, in press) or shared case write-ups with clients, they have all commented on the continued healing that happened for them as they saw the work summarized. I think that this has important implications for how report writing is done in psychotherapy. Currently, it is primarily clinicians that have access to written case materials, which ignores the possibilities for closure, support, and a more collaborative therapist-client relationship that exists within a more open framework.

The main point of difference that emerged between my and the parents' perspective was Matthew's view of my use of the term myth. He fully agreed with the definition which I presented at the beginning of the paper, but felt that as people read the case, they would fall back into the more usual negative definition of the word. His preference would have been to use the word storytelling instead of myth. Rachel felt that the term myth worked for the mythmaking themes that I presented, except for the first theme, the "myth of careful caretaking." She thought this was just a stuck pattern that did not carry with it some of the larger multigenerational and cultural issues that the other three mythmaking themes carried. Also, in discussion with Rachel, it also became clear that the paper highlighted more of the in-session than the out-of-session work. I had more access to the in-session work. She had a number of good things to say about the importance of change for her outside of session on multiple levels: small interactional changes, changes in meaning of events, as well as understanding multigenerational patterns. The importance of change happening on all of these levels was emphasized by Rachel.

In the ten months since treatment ended, things have continued to go well with both sons and each other. They have sought no further intervention for their oldest son and both children are doing well in day care and school. Xavier learned to swim.

NOTE

1. Outside resources are often not searched for or acknowledged enough in family therapy. As Haber (1987) has noted, friends are an untapped area of support.

BIBLIOGRAPHY

Anderson, S.A. & Bagarozzi, D.A. (1983). The use of family myths as an aid to strategic therapy. *Journal of Family Therapy*, 5, 145-154.

Anderson, T. (1987). The reflecting team: Dialogue and meta-dialogue in clinical work. *Family Process*, 26, 415-428.

Bateson, G. (1979). *Mind and nature: A necessary unity*. New York: E.P. Dutton.

Byng-Hall, J. (1973). Family myths used as defense in conjoint family therapy. *British Journal of Medical Psychology*, 46, 239-250.

Cronen, V., Pearce, B. & Tomm, K. (1985). A dialectical view of personal change. In: K. Gergen & K. Davis (Eds.), *The social construction of the person*. Springer-Verlag.

Eliade, M. (1960). *Myths, dreams and mysteries*. New York: Harper & Row.

Feinstein, D. (1979). Personal mythology as a paradigm for a holistic public psychology. *American Journal of Orthopsychiatry*, 49, 198-217.

Ferreira, A.J. (1963). Family myth and homeostasis. *Archives of General Psychiatry*, 9, 457-463.

Freilich, M. (1975). Myth, method and madness. *Current Anthropology*, 16, 207-26.

Gardner, R. (1976). *Dr. Gardner's stories about the real world*. New York: Avon.

Haber, R. (1987). Friends in family therapy: Use of a neglected resource. *Family Process*, 26, 269-281.

Imber-Black, E., Roberts, J. & Whiting, R. (in press). *Rituals and family therapy*. New York: Norton Press.

Irwin, E. & Malloy, E. (1975). Family puppet interview. *Family Process*, 14, 179-191.

Levi-Strauss, C. (1973). *From honey to ashes*. Translated by J. and D. Weightman. New York: Harper & Row.

Keeney, B. (1983). *The aesthetics of change*. New York: Guilford Press.

Keim, I., Lentine, G., Keim, J. & Madanes, C. (1987). Strategies for changing the past. *Journal of Strategic and Systemic Therapies*, 6, 2-17.

Pillari, V. (1986). *Pathways to family myths*. New York: Brunner/Mazel.
Roberts, J. (in press). Use of ritual in 'redocumenting' psychiatric history. In: Imber-Black, E., Roberts, J. & Whiting, R. (Eds.), *Rituals and family therapy*. New York: Norton Press.
Ruthven, K.K. (1976). *Myth*. London: Methuen & Co Ltd.
Selvini-Palazzoli, M., Boscolo, L., Cecchin, L. & Prata, G. (1978). A ritualized prescription in family therapy: Odd days and even days. *Journal of Marriage and Family Counseling*, 4, 3-9.
Steinglass, P. (1978). The conceptualization of marriage from a systems theory perspective. In: T.J. Paolino & B.S. McCrady (Eds.), *Marriage and marital therapy*. New York: Brunner/Mazel.
Turner, V. (1967). *The forest of symbols: Aspects of Ndembu ritual*. Ithaca: Cornell University Press.
Van Gennep, A. (1960). *The rites of passage*. (M. Uizedom & G. Caffee, translators). Chicago: The University of Chicago Press.
Williams, M. (1983). *The velveteen rabbit*. New York: A. A. Knopf.
Wolin, S.J. & Bennett, L.A. (1984). Family rituals. *Family Process*, 23, 401-420.

Personal Myths—In the Family Way

David Feinstein
Stanley Krippner

SUMMARY. This paper offers a cognitive conceptualization of personal mythology, presents a model for working with individual's personal mythology, and considers the integral relationships among personal myths, family myths and cultural myths.

> Myth is the secret opening through which the inexhaustible energies of the cosmos pour into human cultural manifestations.
>
> *Joseph Campbell* (1968, p. 3)

Myth-making, in the sense that we will be using the term "myth," is *the* mechanism by which all human beings construct reality. Rather than being reduced to falsehoods or historically doubtful beliefs, myths are more properly viewed as large, controlling images that organize experience in a manner that provides meaning and arouses motivation. They are as intrinsic to contemporary, sophisticated societies as they were to primitive cultures, although they now appear in more subtle guises, clothed often in the language of technology and material progress. They operate at the personal as well as societal levels and have been described as "the means by which visions and ideals are combined with reality" (Robertson, 1980, p. 346). Since, as fields ranging from modern physics to general semantics have persuasively demonstrated, all constructions of reality are approximations and largely arbitrary in nature, the most pertinent measure of a myth's validity is in terms of how functional or dysfunctional its guidance proves to be, rather than according to some image of its veracity.

Correspondence should be sent to David Feinstein, 777 East Main St., Ashland, OR 97520.

111

The family is the crucible in which the imperatives of genetics and the mythology of a civilization are amalgamated into the unique mythic framework that shapes each person's development. Personal myths are the individual's legacy from the past and a source of guidance and inspiration for the future. They are pregnant with the hopes and the disappointments of prior generations. Operating largely outside of conscious awareness, personal myths are internal structures that organize perceptions, govern emotions, coalesce thoughts, and mediate behavior. Personal myths continually evolve and are responsive to purposeful intervention.

In this paper, we will provide a cognitive conceptualization of personal mythology, present a model for working with an individual's personal mythology, and consider the integral relationships among personal myths, family myths, and cultural myths.

A COGNITIVE FORMULATION OF PERSONAL MYTHS

Piaget (1971) identified three basic types of knowledge: (a) innate knowledge, such as drive and instinct; (b) knowledge of the physical world, which is based on sensory perception; and (c) cognitive structures that are a product of reflective abstraction on the other two. Cognitive structures assume mythic proportions as they begin to address the four issues identified by Joseph Campbell (1983) as the primary domains in which mythic thought functions: the need to comprehend the universe in a meaningful way, the search for a pathway to carry oneself through the succeeding epochs of human life, the desire to establish fulfilling relationships within a social and cultural milieu, and the longing to achieve a sense of participation in the vast wonder and perplexity of the universe.

We define *personal myths* as those cognitive structures that *for the individual* explain the world, guide personal development, and establish a relationship with the mysteries of existence *in a manner analogous to* the way cultural myths carry out those functions for entire societies. This definition emphasizes the analog between the role certain cognitive structures play for the individual and the functions cultural myths meet for an entire society. Personal myths are those cognitive structures that are functionally analogous to cultural myths. And as Marlan (1981) has pointed out, it is not that modern man has become any less mythic, but that he has unconsciously lived the myths of logic and science. These myths unduly restrict the deepening of human consciousness and help to foster the feelings of alienation and "exile" so common in modern times. (p. 227)

Cognitive structures function as templates that give form to perceptions, feelings, and thoughts. By defining personal myths in terms of *cognitive structures*, we can turn to the principles that have been established through the study of cognition in order to better understand how personal myths operate. Investigators have, for instance, found that cognitive structures may be coded verbally or pictorially, may or may not be within the individual's awareness, may be influenced by heredity *and* experience, may operate at various levels of human life, and may change in accordance with lawful principles such as Piaget's concepts of assimilation and accommodation (Feinstein, 1979). Because we are defining personal myths as a class of cognitive structure, these statements hold for personal myths as well.

The view that human behavior and experience are mediated by cognitive structures—that people's responses are reactions not to stimuli but to their interpretations of stimuli—is a central concept of the cognitive trend in modern psychology and the backbone of our clinical approach. As Wilson has noted (1978), "recognizing that cognitions have causal influence . . . highlights the human capacity for self-directed behavior change." In our attempts to synthesize existing cognitive theory with our observations from working with the mythologies of scores of individuals in clinical, educational, and community settings, we have derived eight propositions that summarize our understanding of the way that personal mythologies evolve. While we have elaborated upon these propositions elsewhere (Feinstein, Krippner, & Granger, in press), they are briefly enumerated here:

1. To emerge from the mythic structure in which one has been psychologically embedded, and to move to another integrated set of guiding images and premises, is a natural and periodic phase of personal development.

2. Personal conflicts — both in one's inner life and external circumstances — are natural markers of these times of transition.
3. Unresolved mythic conflicts reemerge, interfering with the resolution of subsequent developmental tasks.
4. The preoperational level of thought described by Piaget is a natural focus of interventions that engage the mythic plane.
5. On one side of underlying mythic conflict will be a self-limiting myth rooted in past experience that is best understood in terms of its constructive purposes in the individual's history.
6. On the other side of the conflict will be an emerging counter-myth that serves as a force toward expanding the individual's personality and prerogatives in the very areas the old myth was limiting them.
7. While this conflict may be painful and disruptive, a natural, though often unconscious, mobilization toward a dialectical resolution of the conflict will also be occurring, ultimately yielding a new mythic image and better integrated mythic premises.
8. Reconciling this new mythic image and these more comprehensive premises with existing attitudes, goals, and life style becomes a vital task in the individual's future development.

From these propositions may be derived a set of interventions for assisting individuals in consciously and actively participating in the development of their own evolving personal mythologies. We have formulated a five-stage model for systematically teaching people to more effective make such interventions in their inner lives. The case history presented in the following section illustrates our approach, and the discussion in the subsequent section details each of the five stages.

MOVING THROUGH A LIFE CRISIS WITH A MYTHIC PERSPECTIVE

Ellen (names and other identifying information have been changed) first sought psychotherapy at age 31, presenting symptoms of anxiety and protests that her unhappiness was unfair as she hadn't "done anything wrong." Her entry into treatment was itself a statement of desperation and despair. She felt she "had to" come for help, but the idea of telling her "deep dark secrets" was so foreign and fearful to her that the thought of therapy was aversive. She had been finding it increasingly difficult to function in her job as a nurse practitioner, and she believed that her anxiety was also affecting her health. She reported that her problems were out of control, and she feared that unless she received some kind of help, she would become so incapacitated that she would not be able to continue to care for her patients or her hospitalized father.

Ellen was the eldest of three girls, born at four year intervals. Her father, a high school coach, and her mother, an art teacher at the same school, were concealed alcoholics. As a result of her parents' absorbing careers, as well as their alcohol dependency, a great deal of responsibility fell upon Ellen for the care of her sisters as well as for housework duties. It was made clear to her that while caring for others brought few immediate pleasures, her duties were a fact of life upon which her parents' approval or disapproval was riding. At an early age, Ellen learned that appearances were of the utmost importance and that it was unacceptable for her to speak openly of her feelings and concerns. As a result, Ellen became a somber, overly-conscientious, and self-contained child.

These traits carried Ellen through her adolescence after her father lost his job for reporting to work in increasing degrees of intoxication. Ellen made no friends in high school, being fearful of asking anybody to come home with her, but she was an excellent, though overly-serious, student. The built-in pressures of "maintaining appearances," coupled with the family's genuine need for "someone to be in charge," shaped her emotional stoicism and premature sense of responsibility.

Ellen became preoccupied with guilt after her mother drove an automobile home from a party while drunk, colliding headlong with another car, killing herself and three other people. Ellen felt that somehow she should have been able to interrupt her mother's drinking habit. When Ellen was 17, her sisters were placed in foster homes despite Ellen's vow to take care of them. As a result, for the first time she could recall, Ellen found herself without responsibility for other people.

Ellen did well in college but dropped out after her sophomore year to marry Todd, a college classmate whose most notable virtue was that he professed great love for her. Todd was a poor student, always seemed to be in some kind of trouble, and frequently asked Ellen for "loans" which were never again mentioned by either of them. Ellen saw great potential in Todd and was certain that with her persistent attention he would be able to make something of himself. About a year into the marriage, Ellen realized that Todd was an alcoholic. After three additional years of unhappy marriage, Todd left her for an older woman who owned a home and a sports car. Four years later, her education completed, Ellen met Bart, director of a social service division of the county. Bart was a picture of the dream husband Ellen had envisioned during her adolescence — good-looking, intelligent, and socially conscious. The fact that he seemed to be interested in her amazed Ellen, and she fell head-over-heels in love for the first time in her life. Bart courted her vigorously, and, also for the first time in her life, she felt as if someone really understood her.

The first year of the marriage was the happiest period of her life to that point. She later reflected, "All my secret dreams had come true. I had a clean, pretty house, someone to do things with, and a sense of myself as a worthwhile person." When Ellen's father was diagnosed as having Alzheimer's disease, Ellen felt compelled to do everything in her power to care for him. She overruled Bart's objections and brought her father into their home. This was too much for Bart, who was already complaining that Ellen's proclivity for self-sacrifice, her obsession with "doing good deeds," and her difficulty in enjoying herself were difficult for him to handle. Their marriage ended on a bitter note. Shortly after their divorce, Ellen realized that she could not care adequately for her father and had him placed in a nursing home. It was at this point that she first presented herself for treatment.

Stage One: Recognizing Conflict in One's Personal Mythology

While Ellen was reserved in her initial sessions and guarded about discussing her problems, she was responsive to activities that utilized guided imagery and psychomotor expression. One of the most powerful experiences for her in the opening phase of treatment was the creation of a "personal shield" adorned with drawings representing different aspects of her life history. Using the motif of "Paradise," "Paradise Lost," and a "Personal Quest" toward "Paradise Regained," the symbolism for each part of her shield emerged from guided fantasy work that explored these dimensions of her inner life. In the "Paradise" portion of her shield, Ellen drew a white house surrounded by a white picket fence, with a bright yellow sun shining on a colorful garden. In the yard, with big smiling faces, were a man, a woman, a girl, and a dog. In the "Paradise Lost" portion of her shield was the same house, in flames, under clouds of smoke, with a large bottle of vodka poised in the sky, pouring fuel onto the flames. In her vision of "Paradise Regained," she saw a sea of exuberant people frolicking in a large open field. She was standing on a hill overlooking them, and she was secretly aware that she was responsible for their great happiness. In the portion of her shield portraying her "Personal Quest," Ellen was dauntlessly attempting to rescue a female figure who was half buried in quicksand. Ellen had no rope or shovel, and as she later explained it, she was acting tirelessly and out of sheer determination. All around were other people who were also trapped in some way and beckoning to her. One was pinned by a landslide at the edge of a sheer cliff; another was caught in the burning house of her "Paradise Lost" image.

It became obvious to Ellen that while she had positioned herself as a tireless caretaker who expected no rewards for her efforts, many of the problems that plagued her were the residue of these pursuits. Where her personal mythology directed her to organize her relationships and her career around almost any opportunity to provide for others, she was increasingly unhappy and having to contend with mounting evidence that this stance was not working well for her. Her guiding mythology was in a turbulent conflict with the feedback that was pouring in from her life experience. She could not give up, nor had she ever considered giving up, her identity as a helper, yet she could not endure the increasing anxiety and diminishing rewards her current life style, so much a reflection of that identity and its underlying mythology, was bringing her.

Stage Two: Bringing Conflicting Myths into Focus

Throughout her life, Ellen realized, she had unconsciously been living out a family myth that had been a theme in her parents' and her sisters' lives as well as her own. She was able to verbalize it as, "The world is a dangerous place that yields little pleasure but demands a great deal of duty. The safest path is to give an appearance of unexceptional (middle-class) normality and to avoid intimacy." To honestly express their feelings to outsiders was deemed unwise as it would make them vulnerable to strangers who might expose the parents' alcoholism as well as the entire family's sense of inadequacy. The result of the "good behavior" prescribed by these mythic injunctions would be the reward of "not attracting trouble." Ellen's personalized version of this guiding family mythology was inaugurated with her eldest-child role as care-giver to her younger sisters and, more subtly, to her parents.

Ellen represented the mythic conflict she had identified in a "Personal Fairy Tale." In Chapter I of her fairy tale, a Princess was living long long ago in a land far far away where an evil spell had been cast upon the King and the Queen and there was great suffering in all the land. The Princess was very sad until one day she figured out how to break the spell. If she could serve others so perfectly and so selflessly that all in the land would smile with irrepressible delight, the curse would be lifted. So the Princess devoted herself untiringly to make everyone happy. But after years and years of her unyielding efforts, the Kingdom still languished in gloom. That was the end of Chapter I. Much of the therapy at this point was devoted to helping Ellen explore the ways her guiding mythology was structuring her perceptions, feelings, and behavior. Various meditative, fantasy, and role-playing techniques provided an opportunity for her to experience the myth's operation in the "here-and-now" of simulated and imaginary situations. She was able to grasp its dimensions and literally "see beyond the edges" of the mythology that was organizing her personal reality. She came to identify, for instance, her vigilant scanning for signs of pain or discomfort or displeasure in other people, her reflexive mobilization to attend to the needs she perceived, the mechanisms by which she kept her own needs and desires outside her awareness, and sub-verbal self-statements such as "If I am worthy, I will be able to make him smile."

Another way of gaining a perspective on the prevailing myth is to identify what we call the "counter-myth." When a prevailing myth has become outdated or is otherwise dysfunctional, a fledgling alternative myth is, in almost all cases, already being formulated, although its development may still be largely outside of conscious awareness. The counter-myth compensates for the limitations of the prevailing myth, although it is generally constructed more with the logic of wish fulfillment than of the reality principle. By the time the counter-myth is well-developed and entering consciousness with some frequency, the prevailing myth and the counter-myth form the basis of two discrete, alternating, competing ego states. While Ellen was still consciously identified with the old myth, the counter-myth was dystonically breaking through often enough to cause considerable psychological discomfort. Just as she was guided to more fully explore the dimensions of her prevailing myth, she was also provided with a series of techniques for helping her bring the counter-myth into greater clarity, representing it in symbols and words, and examining its edges, strengths, and limitations.

The first glimmerings of an emerging counter-myth are often revealed in dreams, fantasies, free association, and "Freudian slips." Ellen was given instruction for observing her dreams and asking them for magical solutions to the problems she had identified in Chapter I of her "Personal Fairy Tale." Before creating Chapter II of her fairy tale, which was to be an allegorical representation of the counter-myth, Ellen reported a dream where she was in a mansion with many servants who attended to her every need and desire. The second chapter of her fairy tale was patterned after this dream. She was in the castle, (characteristically) caring for an owl with an injured wing. When the owl was again healthy and strong, he granted her three wishes as he left the gloomy castle to return to the forest. Her first wish was that the spell would be taken off her father, the King. The second was that the spell would be taken off her mother, the Queen. The third was that she be given whatever her heart desired. Immediately the darkness was lifted from the castle, the King and Queen were again cheerful, and courtiers and jesters looked after the Princess' every wish and whim. But the owl's power to grant wishes would last only as long as the owl continued to live (the instructions for Chapter II of the fairy tale stipulate that while the solutions to the problems of the first chapter may be magical, they will only be temporary). When the owl died, all would return to as it had been. As the Princess began to enjoy her new circumstances the owl's last words to her echoed in her ears: "Observe carefully how your life changes after your wishes are granted, and you will have the key to breaking the spell forever." That was the end of Chapter II.

The counter-myth, as illustrated in the second chapter of Ellen's fairy tale, is usually compensatory and often embodies qualities that are the polar opposites of those found in the prevailing myth. Ellen had never been the recipient of the kind of caretaking she so freely offered, and even when Bart was wanting to give more attention to his wife, she was so busy helping others that she was not able to receive it. Her dream and her fairy tale suggested that at some level she was exploring how life might be if it were governed by a very different controlling image than the one with which she was so deeply identified.

Stage Three: Heading Toward Resolution

Ellen was instructed to name and personify the competing mythic images. "The Invisible Servant," with whom she could easily identify, was guided by the prevailing myth. "The Pampered Princess," an ego state she found detestable, was guided by the counter-myth. Ellen diligently examined the feelings, memories, and self-statements associated with each character and enacted dialogues between the two. In these dialogues, "Princess" assumed a haughty posture and initially demanded that "Servant" stop serving others and use her abundant energy to find others to serve Ellen. "Servant," with shoulders stooped, bent at the waist, and breathing in a labored manner, defended the virtues of uncomplaining service, and then interrupted her argument to (self-mockingly) ask the therapist if she could bring him a drink of water or a cinnamon roll she had in her car. Ellen asked for dreams that would put these two subpersonalities into better communication with one another. Over time, she began to question her caretaking stance and to earnestly consider that she begin to expect more from her relationships with others. Through a series of dialogues over several months, "Servant" and "Princess" began to respect one another's position, started discussing what they needed from one another, and became able to give one another concrete suggestions and support. "Princess," for instance, pointed out that the shame "Servant" felt for ever needing another's caring was keeping her trapped in her role. For her part, "Servant" insisted that as long as "Princess" was so totally selfish, "Servant" would never move an inch toward her side, but the two finally began to consider compromises.

Stage Four: Choosing a Renewed Guiding Mythology

In an exercise where Ellen symbolized her old myth in one side of her body and the counter-myth in the other, she was eventually instructed to have the feelings of the two sides merge and harmonize and to allow an image to emerge that represented a new integration of the two myths. She saw a picture of herself skillfully and joyously navigating a river raft through rapids, with a group of six others on the raft who were totally dependent on Ellen's skill. Ellen had found her few experiences of white water rafting to be thrilling, but had never considered becoming proficient at it. She became captivated with the fantasy that she might use her instinct for taking care of others to guide trips in "white water around the world." She drew the picture of her raft on the fifth portion of her shield, "A Renewed Guiding Image."

Chapter III of the personal fairy tale was to take into account this image, along with dreams where Ellen had requested guidance for resolving the conflict between her competing myths, and the various dialogues and other experiences where she was consciously attempting to foster an integration between the two. In Chapter III of Ellen's fairy tale, the Princess, recalling the owl's last words to her, not only counted her blessings every day, but she also carefully observed all that occurred. After seven seasons of a golden peace, the land again grew very dark, and the Princess knew that the ow had died. She began to take stock of all she had observed. She remembered, for instance, that the servants who were so jovial when attending her seemed very sad when they didn't know anyone was watching them. She had noticed that as every task was done for her and every inconvenience removed, she spent more and more time in bed and did fewer and fewer deeds for herself or for the kingdom. She had realized that where at first she felt rested and elated she soon grew bored and as discontented as the servants. She had noticed that the happiest people in all the land were the craftsmen and women who created beautiful things seemingly for their own enjoyment. She wondered if she could create something just for her own enjoyment. She had always loved stained glass and she apprenticed herself to the master glazier. She found she was quite adept and her work soon gained recognition near and far. She began to travel as more and more of the townsfolk asked her to create stained glass windows in their homes whose images would give them special powers and would brighten their lives. Soon her life was busy and rich and although she was still sad about the King and Queen's unhappiness, she was no longer trapped by the evil spell that had cursed their kingdom. Ellen developed a moral to her fairy tale which also served as a summary of the new myth she was exploring: "If you find what you love to do, you will serve others better than if you aim to serve them."

Stage Five: Weaving the Renewed Mythology into Daily Life

Implementing a mythic statement of this nature is a process that requires a good deal of experimentation and revision. Ellen was taught how to develop personal rituals that involved visualization and behavioral rehearsals. She was shown how to evaluate and rearrange the contingencies in her life in order to better support the new myth. She entered into behavioral contracts that made her accountable for taking incremental steps in the direction of the new myth. One daily ritual she developed was to stand before the mirror each morning with a posture and countenance that expressed the confidence and self-respect of "Princess" along with the compassion and kindness of "Servant." In a tone of voice that captured this integration, she would announce to the image in the mirror her intentions for that day vis-à-vis the new myth.

A contingency change Ellen implemented was to nurture a new type of friendship, one that would be supportive of her new mythology. Her friendships had generally been superficial and one-way, with Ellen, in some manner, assuming the role of helper. Along with sharing her feelings in more depth than she had ever before contacted them, her therapy coincided with her developing a deep friendship with a neighbor named Mary. While Ellen's instinct in many instances was to back off from the friendship, she chose to use it as an experiment in receiving as much as she gave within a relationship. It turned out that Mary also came from an alcoholic family, and the friendship turned into a significant support system for each of them. Another contingency that Ellen changed involved the tremendous amount of time she was giving as a volunteer in a variety of service capacities. In her therapy sessions, she enacted several role-plays of how she, from her new posture, was going to resign from these responsibilities. The guilt and self-recrimination that came up were dealt with by having her focus on their relationship to her old myth. Ellen used part of her newfound time to further develop her friendship with Mary and to take an adult education course on river rafting, and part of it to allow herself to have more moments of private relaxation. A big step for her was to confront her supervisor and announce that she was no longer willing to always take the least desirable shifts and assignments. Several months later she made arrangements to take the summer off, except for occasional fill-in assignments, so she could pursue her new interest in river rafting.

As that summer approached, two years after her first consultation, she cheerfully announced one day that she was ready to terminate treatment. In reviewing the steps she had taken during her therapy, she was able to articulate the change from her self-sacrificing old myth to a stance that allowed more balance in her relationships. She emphasized how much more satisfaction she was deriving from those relationships and how excited she was about pursuing river-rafting for her own enjoyment instead of as a means of serving others. The most significant change for her was that her self-esteem had increased substantially; her basis for liking herself was no longer founded upon the shaky ground of her ability to please others. She recognized that these changes still required monitoring. While the old myth could still get its grips on her, particularly when she was under stress, she was confident that the steps she had taken would carry her in the direction of the new mythology she had so carefully formulated.

A FIVE-STAGE MODEL FOR WORKING
WITH THE INDIVIDUAL'S PERSONAL MYTHOLOGY

The general approach taken with Ellen may be used in working with individuals, families, or workshop groups. In individual and family work, a manual (Feinstein & Krippner, in press) that conducts people through the five-stage process via some 30 exercises, such as drawing the personal shield, is presented for work at home. Weekly therapy sessions are left free to focus on the feelings that emerge in the process, along with their relevance to the individual's past and present life. The manual is completed over several months, but the personal symbolism and constructs that emerge provide a context for ongoing work, which, in the case of individual treatment, typically lasts from 6 to 30 months. In family therapy, children who, because of age of inclination, are not interested in carrying out the exercises, still participate in at-home meetings where other family members share the results of their work. The ensuing discussion about what emerged for their parents and other family members is often startling to them, and it also has the effect of bringing them to consider the personal relevance of the issues being examined.

In weekly psychotherapy, as contrasted with a workshop format, clients move through the process at varying paces and the design is adjusted to fit their unique situation and needs. Because the workshop format is more uniform, we will use it to discuss in greater detail our five-stage model for teaching people to identify and work with their own guiding myths. The workshop requires a minimum of 18 hours. We have presented it as a long weekend, a six-evening course, and a five-day retreat. By the fifth hour, participants have selected a single problematic area of their personal mythology to focus upon for the remainder of the workshop, and, through a sequence of structured experiences, called "personal rituals," systematically begin to transform it.

The workshop begins with a lecture and discussion of the culture's changing myths, with reference to classical mythology, leading to an understanding of our central premises that myths are part of the fabric of modern as well as ancient cultures. Myths operate at a personal as well as collective level, they are the manner by which human beings construct personal reality, and there is thus a mythic basis to all thought, feeling, and behavior. We also explain that the program will utilize didactic instruction, structured rituals, guided imagery, other induced altered states, and ceremonies that employ the group to empower each participant's efforts. As a first step in encountering their own mythic foundations, we have participants go on an inner journey to visit four of their ancestors. Guided visualization is accompanied by facilitative music and physical movement where each individual assumes a posture that represents the ancestor being visited. Participants open their imaginations to envision the mythologies each ancestor lived out, and they consider the consequences each of these scenarios might have had upon subsequent generations. The sequence takes them in a direct line to their own birth, and it helps participants begin to apprehend the mythic ecology into which they were born.

This emerging comprehension of their family's mythology provides a background for understanding their own journey. Any given personal myth may bring out one aspect of the person and inhibit another, and these myths may be useful or destructive. Myths "can engender efforts of Olympian quality, or they may inspire inertia and vindictiveness" (London & Weeks, 1981, p. vii). Families actively select and adopt as their own "those cultural myths whose various components and symbols have meaning and importance for each family member" (Bagarozzi & Anderson, 1982, p. 72). The family is the institution charged with creating a person-sized mythology for each of its young. It has first claim on molding the development of the individual's guiding mythology, and it provides a microcosm as the person unfolds into the wider community (Paub-Bynum, 1984). A commentary from the Chinese *Book of Changes* (the *I Ching*), perhaps the oldest existing book on the planet, portrays the family as "society in embryo":

It is the native soil on which performance of moral duty is made easy through natural affection, so that within a small circle a basis of moral practice is created, and this is later widened to include human relationships in general. (p. 144)

The development of the individual's mythology must be understood against the backdrop of the mythology evidenced in the family of origin.

The "personal shield" described in the presentation of Ellen's material is another structured experience conducted early in the workshop. The shield is divided into five parts, and each section is adorned with a drawing symbolizing a specific aspect of the person's inner journey. These sections are framed in the metaphors of "Paradise," "Paradise Lost," a vision of "Paradise Regained," a personal "Quest" toward that vision, and "A Renewed Vision." The first two sections generally portray experiences with the person's family of origin. As the personal shields are ceremoniously shared and their meanings explored, a commitment is made by the group to use its collective influence for empowering each of the participants on the next steps of the personal journey. The shield is also used in subsequent personal rituals, such as for protection if the inner work becomes too frightening or too painful. The "Renewed Vision" is drawn toward the end of the workshop, incorporating the insights that have been gained into a symbolic representation of a new orientation in the person's inner life.

The central focus of the workshop involves the identification of one area of dysfunction in each participant's guiding mythology and the transformation of that difficulty through principles that correspond with the eight propositions listed earlier. We have found that successfully completing this process even one time can teach people to more effectively work with the mythic dimensions of ongoing experience in subsequent situations. The workshop is organized around the five stages used to present Ellen's work. These stages are congruent with our cognitive formulation of personal mythology, and they have been developed and refined with over 2000 workshop participants. A brief description of each of these stages follows.

First Stage

The objective of the first stage of the model is to help participants identify underlying conflict or dysfunction in their guiding mythology. They begin to examine the myths that are shaping their lives with an eye toward areas that are not serving them well. Myths, functioning properly, may be seen as allies that organize experience in a manner that empowers their holders. People and circumstances change, however, and myths that once served as effective guidance may have become dysfunctional or even destructive. When a personal myth is causing trouble, the psyche will generate alternative cognitive schemas that begin to compete with it. As this occurs, evidence of the conflict will emerge, manifesting in anxieties, phobias, physical symptoms, puzzling dreams, self-contradictions, or feelings of confusion, ambivalence, or dissatisfaction. We view the conflict between an old prevailing myth and an emerging counter-myth as the cutting edge of personal growth.

While the psyche reflexively works to bring conflicting myths toward resolution, with or without conscious attention, the conflict will be more destructive and more likely to engender detrimental defenses when it occurs outside of awareness. Conversely, it is more likely to reach a harmonious and economical resolution that is in line with the person's deeper values when the conflict is worked through with conscious assistance. In this first stage of the workshop, a series of personal rituals is presented for systematically identifying areas of mythic conflict that might lend themselves to constructive resolution. For instance, the symbolism of the shield is examined for areas of mythic tension, a dream is requested that reveals areas of underlying conflict, behavior is ritualistically reviewed for evidence of mythic conflict, and symbolism is finally generated to represent the area of conflict that was ultimately chosen for further focus.

Second Stage

The objective of the second stage of the model is to crystalize the old myth and the counter-myth into explicit words and images. The roots of the prevailing dysfunctional myth are examined, its impact considered, and the emerging counter-myth is explored. The dysfunctional myth that was identified in the first stage had perhaps been the best guidance available in previous life circumstances, but it will have come to perpetuate a tiring theme in the person's life. Its roots will be found in some combination of temperament, early conditioning, experiences with betrayal, trauma, and success, and a unique synthesis of the myths held by family and culture. The counter-myth that challenges the old order may be imaginative, inspiring, and forward-looking, but it will also often lack a practical realism that allows it to be lived out just as the psyche has formulated it.

Bringing focused attention to the conflict between the old myth and the emerging myth allows conscious participation in reaching a resolution that is attuned to the person's developmental needs and best interests. Among the guided instructions offered for productively focusing on both sides of the conflict is a journey back in time to a real or hypothetical instance that may have inaugurated the old myth. As you saw in the case study, the old myth is also transformed into the first chapter of a three-part "Personal Fairy Tale." The emerging myth, which is further examined through dreams and structured imagery experiences, then serves as the basis of the second chapter. The consequences that the old myth and the counter-myth are having on the person's thoughts, feelings, and behavior are also examined.

Third Stage

The objective during the third stage is to mediate the conflict as the opposing myths push toward a natural synthesis. After having identified an area of conflict in one's mythic construction of reality, and having come to understand the roots and the purposes of both sides of that conflict, images of integration become possible. The individual is taught to recognize that facing one's inconsistencies without a retreat into the old or a flight into the emerging may be as difficult as it could be valuable. Sacrificing the familiarity, comfort, and identification with a prevailing though outdated myth can be so painful that some people fight dearly to reject the emerging myth. For others, recognizing areas of dysfunction that are associated with the old myth may be so distressing that they totally disidentify with it and fully embrace the emerging myth.

The challenge in this stage of the work is to give adequate recognition to the messages and purposes of both sides of the conflict. A new mythic image that transcends the old myth and the counter-myth, while achieving a synthesis which embodies the most functional aspects of each can be fostered. The structured activities during this phase of the workshop are designed to reinforce the most beneficial elements of the prevailing myth and integrate them with those of the counter-myth. Among the guided experiences carried out toward these ends is a personification of both myths and the enactment of a dialogue between them. Various other techniques employing visual as well as bodily representations of the conflict and its possible resolution, such as the exercise where Ellen symbolized her old myth on one side of her body and the counter-myth on the other side, are also used.

Fourth Stage

In this stage of the work, the person is called upon to examine the new mythic vision that was synthesized from the dialectic described above and to refine it to the point where a commitment to that vision may be maturely entered. While it is necessary to allow the natural dialectic between the old myth and the counter-myth to take its course, the process may be never-ending, and a time does come when choosing to identify with a carefully refined version of the emerging mythic image can facilitate personal development.

A series of structured experiences lead workshop participants into altered states of consciousness where deeper sources of knowledge become available for examining and crystalizing this emerging mythic image. This may set the directions in which participants consciously begin to reshape their lives. Among the personal rituals that comprise this stage of the workshop are invoking an *inner shaman* to heal emotional wounds that may be impeding one's development (Feinstein, 1987), consulting a "power object" regarding the new guiding image and its refinement, and consulting one's own dreams. The final chapter of the "Personal Fairy Tale," which embodies the newly synthesized guiding myth, is also created during this stage.

Fifth Stage

The fifth stage extends beyond the workshop and involves preparing participants to weave their newly formulated myth into their lives. It requires them to become practical and vigilant monitors of their commitment to achieve a harmony between daily life and the renewed guiding mythology that was formulated during the workshop. The old Hassidic saying that "everyone should carefully observe what way his heart draws him and then choose that way with all his strength" summarizes this final phase. The proverb recognizes that old behavioral patterns, conditioning, and character armoring which were associated with the old myth will tend to persist. Focused attention is required for anchoring even an inspiring new myth that has been wisely formulated.

The workshop closes with a series of structured experiences that lay the groundwork for success in this transition. This final phase draws particularly from techniques that have been developed by cognitive and behavioral therapists for bringing about changes in perception and functioning. Self-statements that support the new myth are formulated, and self-statements that might unwittingly promote the old myth or the counter-myth are identified. Role-plays allow the person to experience acting upon the new myth under simulated conditions. Bodily representations and visual imagery are used to strengthen the chosen myth as a thought form. Behavioral contracts with other group members or the *inner shaman* are also entertained. These contracts focus on changes in the areas of participants' lives that still reinforce the myth they are wanting to transform, as well as on changes in areas that do not yet reinforce the mythic image they are wanting to pursue. Back-home ceremonies that inaugurate the new myth and daily rituals that reinforce it and re-establish contact with the mythic realm are also suggested.

PERSONAL AND FAMILY MYTHS
IN A CONTEMPORARY CONTEXT

Personal myths and family myths pitch and float upon the changing tides of the broader culture's mythology. The single overwhelming trend affecting the mythologies of contemporary cultures is change itself. The requirements for adjusting and thriving are fluctuating exponentially faster than in any previous sustained period of history. The guiding myths of the parents' generation are in many ways not even remotely fitting for the needs of the day. Not only are the vicissitudes of life shifting at a dizzying pace, but the family, the culture's durable touchstone for maintaining a sense of orientation and security within changing circumstances, has been in whirling chaos as well. In the 1950s, 70 percent of all American households consisted of a "typical" family constellation of a wage-earning father, a stay-at-home mother, and one or more children; two decades later, this "typical" American family accounted for only 15 percent of the households (Yankelovitch, 1981). The alleged "death of the family" has been a frequent topic of modern commentators, and, even if the proverbial cradle has not fallen, it is at least rocking very rapidly.

The seeds of the family's future direction are contained in the mythic motifs pushing for expression in contemporary societal developments. A mythically-informed psychology allows themes that will be playing themselves out on the social plane to be anticipated, understood, and influenced. The remaining discussion is presented with the conviction that clinicians and educators who work with families are pressed to attune themselves to the mythic tides that buoy changing social conditions. A perspective that remains cognizant of such often unperceived influences results in a more penetrating understanding of the cultural dynamics that are at the foundation of clinical situations. A mythically-informed clinical attitude leads to therapeutic interventions that, rather than "pathologizing" (Hillman, 1975), account for and effectively confront the fundamental cultural tensions that contribute to maladjustment. Three underlying forces in contemporary society that are of particular significance to the mythic life of the family and its members are mentioned here.

1. The Development of Consciousness as the Personalizing of Mythology

The historical record suggests that the self-reflecting individual is a relatively recent development in social evolution, having appeared as a mass phenomenon perhaps only as recently as within the past thirty-five hundred years (Wilber, 1981). In earlier eras, the sense of self was fully identified with the body and the primordial forces of nature. Consciousness later became differentiated from the physiological life of the body, but it was still immersed in the experiential life of the communal group (Wilber, 1981). As civilization advanced, complexity increased, and societies became ever more differentiated. People constructed their experiential worlds in increasingly unique ways. The mythologies that had been so tightly bound to consensual reality within the homogenous group began to burst as they were distended by the joint onslaught of burgeoning social progress and individualistic interpretation. The burden of constructing an intelligible mythology — for explanation, guidance, and connection with the community and with the cosmos — fell to an unprecedented extent upon the shoulders of the individual.

This emerging individuality required a completely new way of thinking. A self-observing aspect of the psyche had come into being. This led to the differentiation of a separate ego, and the individual's identity surfaced from its total immersion in the community and into the anxious solitude that characterizes many modern individuals. Campbell (1968) has observed that in primitive times "all meaning was in the group" while today "all meaning is in the individual" (p. 388). From a mythological perspective, we could say that the essential trend in the development of human consciousness in recent millennia has been the personalizing of mythology. Thus one trend which clinicians and educators must understand when bringing a mythic perspective to family life is that individuals are increasingly challenged to consciously participate in charting their own guiding mythologies. Family and cultural myths have been losing their currency as the final arbitrators of personal reality, and as much as this may be disorienting for the individual, it may also be a source of confusion for therapists who have not fully examined the relationship of their clinical assumptions to the prevailing myths of their culture.

2. Idolatry of the Ego

The emergence of the individual ego allowed previously unimagined possibilities — the capacities for psychological autonomy, self-reflection, and a measure of objectivity — but it did not come without substantial costs. As consciousness emerged from the body and became distinguished from that of the social group, the Cartesian dualism that has plagued modern society had become full-blown. Neumann (1954) has noted that "our cultural unease or dis-ease is due to the fact that the separation of the systems (ego and instinct) — in itself a necessary product of evolution — has degenerated into a schism and thus precipitated a psychic crisis whose catastrophic effects are reflected in contemporary history" (p. 363).

The inspirational cultural myths of times past have become fragmented, twisted, impotent, or dead, and humanity has become cut off from the mythic realm that might provide nourishment and sustenance. Many thinkers have identified the difficulties inherent in the overvaluation of the rational mind. London and Weeks (1981) noted that "in our own age, we have become so enamoured of allegedly 'rational' ideas buttressed by scientific logic and empirical 'evidence' that we intentionally debunk myths, or we replace the ones that were seemingly irrational with 'new' rational ones" (p. xiii). The Western ego has been overly identified with the rational, individualistic side of existence while mythology is integrally related to the primordial and the communal. The ego has identified its own rationality as the final arbitrator of reality, and the great mythic forces of the psyche have been suppressed, disembodied, and relegated to realms outside the individual's conscious awareness. While rationality has been the ego's strength, the ego's blind spots have proliferated as civilization has become progressively separated from nature. Effective therapists must understand the proportions of this conflict between rationality and deeper intuitive forces and must be able to identify the subtle ways that an individual's or a family's mythology may be geared toward systematically suppressing certain affects in the service of a particular image of rationality.

3. The Democratization of Gender Relationships

The dominating myth in recent history has been the hero's journey, which at the psychological level reflects the emergence of the self-conscious, freely-willing, patriarchal personal ego. Campbell (1968) has noted that "the standard path of the mythological adventure of the hero is a magnification of the form represented in the rites of passage: *separation — initiation — return*" (p. 30). The problem with the modern heroic journey is that while past mythologies still provide abundant imagery for the heroic *separation*, extant maps for the heroic *return* no longer match the terrain. The great hero myths traditionally included a voluntary or forced exile from one's culture, but "myths of 'exile' made no sense without myths of return and renewal, myths that promise an alliance with the ground of being" (Marlan, 1981, p. 227). Without the sense of completion that these myths offer, modern men and women can be described as having "lost their way" and as seeking in vain to return to "the right path" (p. 227).

Several trends in modern history are implicated in the unprecedented estrangement between heroic separation ventures and viable images of a return. The industrial age has forced upon individuals an increasing degree of separation from both nature and community. In addition, the development of individualism has made the heroic journey a common rather than elite path in modern Western cultures (Bellah, Madsen, Sullivan, Swidler, & Tipton, 1985). Thus, the home to which the alienated hero longs to return is no longer populated with a community poised to greet the returning hero and welcome his or her gifts. These developments both require and make possible new types of social arrangements that would have been inconceivable prior to the individualization of consciousness. A prototype of the hero's return from classical mythology is Odysseus, who had fought valiantly in the Trojan War. His return, as told in Homer's *The Odyssey*, is fraught both with hazards—the Lotus-Eaters, the Cyclops, the Sirens—and delights—Circe, Calypso, Nausicaa. Through strength and cunning, Odysseus finds his way back to his kingdom Ithaca, his wife, Penelope, and their son, Telemachus. He has been away for two decades. Odysseus, representing the eternal quest of the male hero, has longed for Penelope and his homeland throughout his journey. Homer tells us that for Odysseus, Penelope is like "the sunwarmed earth" that is "longed for by a swimmer spent in rough waters where his ship went down." Odysseus and Penelope's marriage bed had been rooted to the earth, with an olive tree serving as a bedpost, and his unsevered attunement with nature throughout his journey had paved the road to his return.

But classic mythic images of the hero's return do not fit the plight of modern heroes. With the rise of the self-conscious ego, the hero's journey became everyone's venture. Unlike Odysseus, contemporary heroes have lost their connection with the natural order, and because their homeland is now populated by other disconnected heroes, their formative experiences in the home are in separation from community as well. Odysseus was a singular hero, returning alone, to a family who awaited his return. In the contemporary era, all people seem engaged in the challenges of the personal heroic journey. The modern Penelope, rather than waiting at home for 20 years, is likely to be on her own heroine's journey as the homefires flicker unattended.

Despite these differences, there are also lessons to be learned from *The Odyssey's* finale. Odysseus returned to find that suitors had not only laid claim to Penelope, they had plundered his house, decimated his provisions, disposed of his resources, and made plans to murder his son and steal his inheritance. Odysseus dramatically challenges the suitors and reclaims his wife, his kingdom, and his land. Humanity in modern times has wantonly misused the earth's resources and placed the inheritance of future generations in jeopardy. The overriding demand facing today's returning hero requires, in the tradition of Odysseus, cleansing a home fouled by unrestrained avarice, putting the household in order, and reinstating the children's birthright to the world's assets. The new hero's challenge is unique in the way it requires both individual ingenuity and collective effort.

The evolution of democracy has been a vital response to the hero's journey having become a quest of the masses rather than the solitary individual. We are speaking of democracy here, not in a narrow political sense, but in terms of a broad recognition of the right and ability of individuals to participate in the decisions that affect their destiny. From a mythological perspective, democracy may be defined as a social arrangement where the group collaboratively chooses the mythic visions that are to be collectively embraced. Democracy as a cultural form allows a collectivity of heroes and heroines to form communities that are attuned to the pluralistic needs of freely-willing egos. Democratic social arrangements provide a necessary counter-balancing to the increased independence that has accompanied the historical personalizing of mythology. Democratization may, in fact, be seen as the propelling force underlying such social developments as the women's movement and the resulting turbulence in gender relationships and family roles. Neumann (1954) believed that while in the past, individuals endowed with greatness "possessed a consciousness and stood for the collective in the role of leader," the further course of evolution must involve "a progressive democratization, in which a vast number of individual consciousnesses work productively at the common human task" (p. 434).

Modern cultures are populated by a plethora of highly individuated heroes and heroines in an increasingly interdependent world, and democratic social organization is the most viable path yet cut if the mythic journey is to lead to a recovery of the sacrificed connections with the human community. While Western democracies are marred by their competitiveness, alienation, and inequalities of opportunity, trends toward increased participation, decentralization, and connectedness have also been identified (Naisbitt, 1982). As recently as the 1960s, patriarchal rule was still generally assumed for the family and the workplace even in Western nations which espoused the ideals of democracy in their political system. The women's movement adamantly challenged those assumptions. Whereas male myths have focused upon the tasks of *separation*, female myths have typically been more concerned with connectedness and may thus point the way in the as yet uncharted *return* of the contemporary hero.

Whether in times of stability or upheaval, the family has served as a robust institution for comforting the patriarch who was trapped in the separation phase of the hero's quest. Even while alienated from nature and the larger community, the family provided him a consoling sense of home and connectedness. Now, however, "the basic building block of the society is shifting from the family to the individual" (Naisbitt, 1982, p. 233). The recent turbulence in family structures and in gender identity can be seen as reverberations of democratic tendencies finding expression at the individual level. The upheaval in the traditional family came with such uncanny speed and force that it almost seemed a collective response to some invisible undertow. Waves of change that are catalyzed by deeper shifts in the culture's mythos may often be characterized in that manner. Pogrebin (1983) has argued that the traditional patriarchal family is democracy's "original sin"; it is the elemental flaw in an otherwise perfectible political system. . . . Very simply, it is impossible to achieve the exalted goals of the democratic dream and the free and full development of every person so long as the basic unit of our society, the family, is undemocratic and unfree. (pp. 18-19)

Available evidence from studies of contemporary families does indeed suggest that the happiest marriages are egalitarian, while marriages typified by one partner's domination are correlated with marital dissatisfaction (Gray-Little & Burks, 1983). In the pre-democratic marriage of the 1950s and earlier, each partner's commitment was toward fulfilling a prescribed set of gender-linked role expectations. In the marriages that seem to be evolving today, the commitment is increasingly toward the integrity of a relationship between equals. Before the dawning of the individualized ego, autocratic rule was a logical arrangement for social relationships. While its vestiges still remain in families and governments, it is becoming outmoded for modern individuals. Pogrebin (1983) has emphasized that "just as the authoritarian family is the authoritarian state in microcosm, the democratic family is the best training ground for life in a democracy" (p. 18). No perfect form of democracy has ever existed on the planet. Not only was Athens a major slave market, but its women lacked citizenship and the right to vote. Members of contemporary democracies frequently live with an interlocking conformity and isolation which pervert the ideal of the form. It may well be that the steps of democratizing marriage and equalizing gender relationships are required before the next turn in the evolution of democracy may be accomplished.

Clinical Implications of These Trends in Contemporary Mythology

One of the great embarrassments for the psychotherapy establishment is the hand it unwittingly lent in suppressing the brewing discontent among women in the late 1950s and 1960s. By reframing the complaints of their female clients, therapists served as a force to literally keep women in their place as second class citizens with unfulfilling roles and limited opportunities. Such therapists, by focusing on their clients' failure to adjust to the existing role expectations, were acting within their training but were oblivious to the mythic conflict that was about to take center stage in the societal arena. Neumann (1969) has observed that

> not infrequently a sensitive person falls ill because of his incapacity to deal with a problem which is not recognized as such by the world in which he lives, but which is, in fact, a future problem of humanity which has confronted him and forced him to wrestle with it. (p. 29)

People whose difficulties lead them to seek psychiatric consultation are often sensitive to underlying cultural conflicts, and it is incumbent upon those who would assist them to be attuned to the mythological layer of their personal suffering. The woman who is torn between her desire to express her individuality in a career and the demands she faces as wife and mother reflects a battle that is being waged within the culture's mythology. A young man unable to settle on a career direction can be helped by coming to understand the mythological reasons for the culture's poverty of heroes and the impact of this situation upon his self-concept and sense of direction. A family whose unity is being destroyed by an adolescent's acting out behavior may come to understand the mythic proportions of the conflict between individuality and relationship and begin to respond to these deeper issues.

The approach presented in this paper develops in the client an understanding of mythic processes at the personal, familial, and cultural levels. As people learn to identify and effectively work with their own personal myths, they become able to find personally relevant resolutions of broader cultural conflicts within the microcosm of their own lives.

REFERENCES

Bagarozzi, D. A., & Anderson, S. (1982). The evolution of family mythological systems: Considerations for meaning, clinical assessment, and treatment. *Journal of Psychoanalytic Anthropology, 5,* 71-90.
Bellah, R. N., Madsen, R., Sullivan, W. M., Swidler, A., & Tipton, S. M.

(1985). *Habits of the heart: Individualism and commitment in American life*. Berkeley: University of California Press.

Campbell, J. (1968). *The hero with a thousand faces* (2nd ed.). Princeton, NJ: Princeton University Press.

Campbell, J. (1983). *Historical atlas of world mythology* (Vol. 1). San Francisco: Harper & Row.

Feinstein, D. (1979). Personal mythology as a paradigm for a holistic public psychology. *American Journal of Orthopsychiatry, 49*, 198-217.

Feinstein, D. (in press). The shaman within: Cultivating a sacred personal mythology. In S. Nicholson (Ed.), *Shamanism*. Wheaton, IL: Quest Books.

Feinstein, D., & Krippner, S. (in press). *Personal mythology*. Los Angeles: J.P. Tarcher, Inc.

Feinstein, D., Krippner, S., & Granger, D. (in press). Myth-making and human development. *Journal of Humanistic Psychology*.

Gray-Little, B., & Burks, N. (1983). Power and satisfaction in marriage: A review and critique. *Psychological Bulletin, 93*, 513-538.

Hillman, J. (1975). *Re-visioning psychology*. New York: Harper & Row.

The I Ching or Book of Changes (R. Wilhelm, & C. F. Baynes, Trans.), (1967). Princeton, NJ: Princeton University Press.

London, H.I., & Weeks, A.L. (1981). *Myths that rule America*. Washington, DC: University Press of America.

Marlan, S. (1981). Depth consciousness. In R.S. Valle & R. von Ekartsberg (Eds.), *The metaphors of consciousness* (pp. 225-242). New York: Plenum.

Naisbitt, J. (1982). *Megatrends*. New York: Warner.

Neumann, E. (1954). *The origins and history of consciousness* (R.F.C. Hull, Trans.). Princeton, NJ: Princeton University Press.

Neumann, E. (1969). *Depth psychology and a new ethic* (Translated by Eugene Rolfe). New York: Harper & Row.

Paub-Bynum, E.B. (1984). *The family unconscious: An invisible bond*. Wheaton, IL: Theosophical Publishing House.

Piaget, J. (1971). *Biology and knowledge: An essay on the relations between organic regulations and cognitive process*. Chicago: Chicago University Press.

Pogrebin, L.C. (1983). *Family politics: Love and power on an intimate frontier*. New York: McGraw-Hill.

Robertson, J. O. (1980). *American myth, American reality*. New York: Farrar, Straus & Giroux.

Wilber, K. (1981). *Up from Eden: A transpersonal view of human evolution*. Garden City, NY: Anchor.

Wilson, T. G. Cognitive behavior therapy: Paradigm shift or passing phase? In J. B. Forcyth & D. P. Rathjen (Eds.), *Cognitive behavior therapy: Research and applications*. New York: Plenum.

Yankelovitch, D. (1981). *New rules: Searching for self-fulfillment in a world turned upside down*. New York: Bantam.

Reality and Myth in Family Life: Changes Across Generations

Frederick S. Wamboldt
Steven J. Wolin

SUMMARY. A theory of mate selection and premarital behavior based upon partners' family myths is presented. Preliminary data from a research project which tested this theory is discussed along with hypotheses regarding the prognosis for couples who assume different postures in relation to their family myths.

From birth on we are engaged in a never ending struggle to convince ourselves that we truly are in control of our lives. Much of this struggle is accomplished within the groups we join during life, for it is in these groups that explanations are created to maximize what is familiar in life and to minimize our surprises. As individuals we internalize the group's explanations and come to accept these constructions as "reality."[1] The explanations of the first group we enter, our family of origin, contributes heavily to the reality on

Frederick S. Wamboldt, MD, and Steven J. Wolin, MD, are affiliated with the Center for Family Research, Department of Psychiatry and Behavioral Sciences, George Washington University Medical Center.

Address correspondence to Dr. Frederick Wamboldt, Center for Family Research, George Washington University Medical Center, Ross Hall, Room 613, 2300 Eye Street, N.W., Washington, DC 20037.

This research has been supported by grants from the National Institute of Mental Health, Physician Scientist Award #5K11-MH00607 (to FSW), and from the Still Water Foundation (to SJW).

1. For simplicity's sake, from here on lower-case reality will be used instead of the enquoted form, "reality," to refer to these shared explanations developed by families and other groups, and upper-case REALITY on those occasions when we need to refer to the "really real."

which we later rely. While this reality is very resistant to change, on occasions subsequent experience can alter our explanations. Marriage is one of the most important of these subsequent reality-evolving experiences, in part because we can choose our partner.

Based on two ongoing research programs, one exploring family of origin influences on early marital development, the other evaluating family influences on the intergenerational transmission of alcoholism, in this paper we propose that both the explanations of reality that a person takes from his or her family of origin and the reworking or transformation of that reality that is accomplished in later life are important determinants of marital health. In particular, we will focus on mate selection and early marriage as a crucial step that individuals take in positioning themselves vis-à-vis their families' explanations. We now enter the thicket, beginning with some definitions.

MYTH AND REALITY

The term *family myth* is used in several different ways. Two major areas of imprecision exist — the first involves issues of distortion and veracity, the second the level where family myth resides. This first area of imprecision is reflected in the two definitions of myth found in more general usage. On one hand, myth is defined as any *explanatory* story with a historical or traditional basis. Hence the alive, dynamic, shared group perception that simultaneously integrates and interprets a family's history, predicts future occurrences and serves as the organizational template for the current interactional behavior of the family's members, frequently is defined as a family's myth — although we prefer to call this a family's *shared construction of reality*, or more simply, their reality. At least equally common is the definition of myth as a *fictitious* story. Under this second definition, the family's myth is seen as necessarily containing a falsification; the clinician's job is to discover and correct the family's "error."

The second area of imprecision in the use of the term, family myth, concerns where the myth is located. Although the significance of this area of imprecision is much greater than the first, the distinction we shall make is much more subtle and, accordingly, more difficult to grasp. On one hand, a family myth is often discussed as a *family-level* phenomenon that cannot be reduced to the composite views, values, or behaviors of the individual family members. The family's reality, which we defined above as the shared perception that integrates the family's past, anticipates their future and coordinates their present, we specifically locate on such a family-level.

Research at our institution has suggested that any family's shared reality contains two especially important, interrelated, explanations. The first is what Reiss (1981) has labeled the *family paradigm* — those shared perceptions within a family concerning the nature of the world outside the family and the place of the family within that world. This explanation serves to answer questions such as, "How does the world work?" and "What is the place of our family in this world?" Bennett, Wolin and McAvity (in press) have described a second dimension of a family's reality as the *family identity* — referring to the current experiential gestalt that arises from the constellation of roles and relationships among family members present during family interaction. The central question here is "Who are we as a family?" These two dimensions are of course simply two different facets of a common shared explanation of the family's reality — one directed "outside" the family (paradigm) and one looking "within" (identity), nonetheless, examining each gives us a slight different vantage of the family's reality.

What is most important is that these explanations are viewed as family-level phenomena. Reiss (1981) has detailed the empirical grounding of his notion of family paradigm in nearly two decades of well-integrated, observational studies exploring how families interact with their environment. Interestingly, his laboratory measurement of a family's paradigm can not be explained solely as a composite of the intellectual, perceptual, and personality attributes of the individual family members (Oliveri & Reiss, 1981; Reiss & Klein, 1987) — in other words, his laboratory procedure seems to measure a *family-level* phenomenon.

In a similar vein, Wolin and colleagues (Bennett et al., in press; Bennett, Wolin, Reiss & Teitelbaum, 1987; Wolin, Bennett, Noonan & Teitelbaum, 1980) have demonstrated that families, who *as a group* regularly insulate and preserve their key family rituals, such as holiday celebrations and daily meals, from the invasive, potentially subsuming, threat of a family member's alcoholism, effectively protect the next generation from the reemergence of alcoholism in another family member. Furthermore, they have argued persuasively that this transgenerational effect occurs because the family that preserves its key rituals permits a healthier, nonalcoholic, family identity to be maintained ("We are an efficacious, resilient family" rather than "Our family has been destroyed, corrupted – our family is weak, ill" or even "Alcohol is part of our family's lifeblood.").

We prefer the label family reality over family myth specifically because on the family-level there is no REALITY (or even sense of potentially different reality) that can be compared to the family's reality and imply distortion or fictitiousness – only within individuals is such recognition of difference possible. More simply put, only individuals can talk and tell us their story – with the inevitable "subjective" shading of the "objective" rules of their reality. This view is consistent with the perspectives of symbolic interactionalism in social psychology and sociology (Mead, 1934; Stryker, 1981) and social constructivism in family therapy (Bateson, 1972; Coyne, 1985; Selvini-Palazzoli, Boscolo, Cecchin & Prata, 1980; Watzlawick, Weakland & Fisch, 1974) which accept that (1) the meaning of life events is derived and modified through social transaction, (2) given different patterns of family transaction, differing realities may arise, and (3) it is at least more clinically useful, and quite possibly even more globally accurate, to view these differences less in terms of better or worse, correct or false, and more as equally valid nuances to be understood because of their central role as determinants of family health.

Conversely, family myth frequently is located on an *individual-level* – namely, to describe the recollections, perceptions, and interpersonal tendencies that individuals internalize or otherwise take away as a result of their being steeped in their families' reality. Byng-Hall's (1982) discussion of his personal revision of a Byng family legend is a nice example of locating family myth on the individual-level. As Byng-Hall astutely notes, different members of the same nuclear family (as well as relatives in more distant branches of the family tree) may have family myths that need not be in precise agreement. We prefer to use the term family myth only on this individual-level because it is here and only here that both of the above-mentioned connotations implied by the word myth, namely, explanation and distortion, truly hold, since only individuals are biologically capable of perceiving, and therefore expressing, the difference between their family's reality and any other reality (let alone REALITY). Therefore, we use family myth to refer to the map or template of the family-level reality, which presently resides within the individual family member, and which may be more or less different from the family's reality because individuals can and do experience the world outside their family.

In summary, we define *family reality* to be an objective group-level construction that organizes a family's experience and coordinates their actions. As such it can not be discussed in words, it can only be inferred through observation of the family's behavior. A *family myth* is a characteristic of individuals, their story of their family. The family myth is seen as being influenced schematically by the family reality, yet being personalized to some degree within each family member as the result of differential life experiences.

Shortly, we will discuss how these differences in the family myths of individual family members have important implications for change in the family's reality, but first, we will propose how families create their reality.

SHARED EXPLANATIONS ORIGINATE IN TRANSACTION, SUSTAIN INTERACTION

The shared explanations of reality that families form arise only during transaction, not during all interaction. Expanding slightly Dewey and Bentley's (1949) distinction, we suggest that given the proper context, interaction between people becomes a *transaction*, in which the participants undergo internal change during the interaction, with each person becoming interdependent with/on the others, modifying each others' beliefs, values, behavior and emotional state through recursive feedback. The proper context that differentiates transaction from mere interaction is best envisioned as one that allows the development of what has been called a "face to face encounter" (Cooley, 1909; Reiss, 1981) or "presence" (Marcel,

1956), in which each person's definition of reality and the associated emotions come under scrutiny and hence are put on the line. As the existentialists have quite clearly noted not all interactions between people are transactions—we all daily encounter a variety of more or less "faceless encounters," e.g., moving in the crowd on the subway or checking out your groceries with the clerk at the store, which are merely patterned interaction and during which transaction does not arise. A bit of introspection is likely to reveal that even among family and loved ones, many everyday encounters are "faceless."

A family's reality as we have defined it, is an alive, dynamic construct, involving a complex relationship between transaction, interaction and family explanation. Any family's reality arises as an epiphenomenon from their transaction, in a manner analogous to how a magnetic moment arises from the spinning electrons in an atom. However once formed, their reality, like the magnetic moment, tends to coordinate/stabilize future interactional behavior along lines similar to that which has previously occurred. Such symbolically dense, "patterned interaction" is one form of repetitive or ritualized behavior seen in families. Additionally, important transactional encounters are frequently repeated as larger scale family rituals which revitalize and reinforce the shared family reality (see Wolin & Bennett, 1984, for an indepth discussion of family ritual, and Bennett et al., in press, for a detailed report of an ethnic family's ritual that is retained over generations).

The importance of our proposed distinction between transaction and interaction is this; it suggests the way in which a family reality once formed can be altered, namely through another, differing, "face to face" encounter. Since transaction is not necessarily limited to occurring only among family members, the transactions outside the family that members have represent the major "window of vulnerability" of the family reality.

REALITY MEETS THE WORLD

Kuhn's (1970) discussion on changes in the working paradigm, or shared explanatory model, of science proposes that such changes are triggered by a surprising discovery, i.e., the bit of data that does not neatly fit into the paradigm's reality. Galileo's discovery of *movement* in several "stars" that were *fixed* in the heavens by Copernican reality, led to his proposing a new reality in which these "stars" were transformed into moons rotating around Jupiter, and the Sun, not the Earth, became the rotational center of the universe. The interpersonal equivalent of such a surprising discovery would arise in what we have labeled transaction. Consider, for example, the changed family myth of the research subject who reported, "My father was an alcoholic, but I never knew it until my wife developed a drinking problem and we both went to AA."

While such surprising discoveries can and do arise in "face to face" encounters throughout the life span of a family, they typically are not evenly distributed across time. With advancing age one's children become much more likely to enter into such relationships. Because of this, any given family's reality is likely to be related to the normative family developmental cycle. More specifically, we propose that a family's reality is generally at its apex of consolidation during the early years of children's lives (when, by contrast, the family myths of individual members will be least different from one another). During this developmental stage, the family, especially the marital dyad, typically has come to consensus (or as close as they will come to consensus) on a number of issues: e.g., how to incorporate their children and the grandparents in the marital twosome, how family members relate to each other and those outside the family, how conflicts of interest within the family are resolved. Additionally, rituals of daily living (e.g., mealtimes, reunions after school and work) as well as larger scale rituals (e.g., birthdays, holiday celebrations) usually have stabilized. In other words, we hold that a more fundamental consensus has been reached — the new family formed in marriage has solidified as a group through the construction of their own reality (In *The Alcoholic Family*, Steinglass, Bennett, Wolin and Reiss [1987] present an extended discussion of such developmental changes in family life).

As the children grow and spend increasing time interacting with an ever enlarging social sphere at play, school and later work, the transactional encounters that arise outside the family frequently act as significant perturbations, placing pressure on the family's reality by "personalizing" the family myths of each member. Consider the second grader, who comes home for dinner and asks to be excused from the family table to watch television, because last evening she and her friend, Lisa, were allowed to do so when she ate at Lisa's house. As Sullivan (1953) described in rich detail, the sharing of "secret views" and joint rehashing of daily events are major elements of the "chumships" of late childhood and adolescence — such conversational sharing of realities not uncommonly leads to surprising discoveries. This process of accumulating surprising discoveries through nonfamily intimacies and thereby personalizing one's family myth, continues into late adolescence and early adulthood and reaches its culmination in the choice of a marital partner.

THE WORLD MEETS THE MYTH

Of course, Galileo's tale does not end with his reconstruction of reality, but continues with his recanting his discovery under social and religious pressure. Similarly, it is unlikely that a single (or even a collection of) "face to face" encounter(s), no matter how earth-shaking, will necessarily change a family's reality, even though the family myth of the individual member who experienced the discovery may have been altered. Something more is required.

Coyne's (1985) football game example nicely highlights this something. Consider the "rules" of football as a social construction, or in our terms, a group reality, i.e., an embodiment of the history of the transactions between participants. Although these rules on one hand are *merely* a social construction, a consensual epiphenomenon, as a group-level phenomenon they are quite durable — the quarterback, who late in the third quarter decides that he will change these socially constructed rules so that by passing the ball through the goal posts he will checkmate the other team and win the game, is unlikely to succeed, precisely because the reality he is trying to change is not his alone, it is held by a group. During the big game, it makes little difference if yesterday he played football with another group who had allowed such a checkmate. The reality will not change unless the group is open to the individual's discovery.

There appear to be rare occasions when families are open to such revisions. While our knowledge of these important change processes remains rudimentary, two central characteristics of such occasions are: (1) the family jointly has struggled with a challenge or crisis that it has not been able to resolve using the explanations inherent in its current reality, (2) family members acknowledge that as a group they (and hence their reality) have not succeeded. Then and only then is radically different information from individual family members likely to become available to the family as a whole (see Reiss, 1981 for a discussion of the passage of families, during an insoluble crisis, from one paradigm to another). However, much more frequently an individual's attempts to revise the family's reality based on his/her discovery is rejected or disconfirmed by the family.

As a result of accumulating these surprising discoveries and attempting to integrate them into the reality of their families, individuals entering their young adult years typically will have evaluatively positioned themselves vis-à-vis their family myths – there will be parts of their family experience that they hold dear, and there will be parts that they intend to change as soon as they have their chance. This chance, of course, comes with marriage – the new couple can rework their family myths – not necessarily within the family they are leaving but rather by constructing a new reality in the family they form.

MYTH MEETS MYTH

In a conceptually rich paper entitled, *Marriage and the Construction of Reality*, Berger and Kellner (1964) describe marriage as a drama in which individuals must redefine both themselves and their world:

> The chief protagonists of the drama are two individuals, each with a biographically accumulated and available stock of experience. As members of a highly mobile society, these individuals have already internalized a degree of readiness to redefine themselves and to modify their stock of experience, thus bringing with them considerable psychological capacity for entering new relationships with others. . . . (Although) the two individuals have internalized the same overall world, includ-

> ing the general definitions and expectations of the marriage
> relationship itself . . . these relatively empty projections now
> have to be actualized, lived through and filled with experien-
> tial content by the protagonists. This will require a dramatic
> change in their definitions of reality and of themselves. (p. 10)

While the influences of the respective families of origin are conspicuously absent from this paper, their views expressed in a later
work (Berger & Luckmann, 1966) clarify that they see the family of
origin as a key determinant of the reality (or in our terms, myth) that
one brings into marriage.

In our terms, new realities are constructed out of transactions.
For Berger and Kellner (1964), this transaction is described as
"conversation":

> Take a simple and frequent illustration – the male partner's
> relationship with male friends before and after the marriage. It
> is a common observation that such relationships, especially if
> the extra-marital partners are single, rarely survive the mar-
> riage, or, if they do, are drastically redefined after it. This is
> typically neither a deliberate decision by the husband nor de-
> liberate sabotage by the wife. What rather happens, very sim-
> ply, is a slow process in which the husband's image of his
> friend is transformed as he keeps talking about this friend with
> his wife. Even if no actual talking goes on, the mere presence
> of the wife forces him to see his friends differently. . . . This
> difference will enter into the joint image that now must be
> fabricated in the course of the ongoing conversation between
> the marriage partners – and, in due course, must act power-
> fully on the image previously held by the husband. Again, this
> process is rarely apprehended with any degree of lucidity. The
> friend is more likely to fade out of the picture by slow degrees,
> as new kinds of friends take his place. . . . This process of
> conversational liquidation is especially powerful because it is
> onesided – the husband typically talks with his wife about his
> friend, but *not* with his friend about his wife. Thus the friend
> is deprived the defense of, as it were, counter-defining the

relationship. This dominance of marital conversation over all others is one of its most important characteristics. (p. 11-12)

At the start of a new relationship, each individual enters with a definite posture towards the family myth they took away from their family reality. As the couple articulates and integrates their respective positions vis-à-vis their origin families, through this transactional process of conversation, they begin to form the group-level reality of their new family.

The "Relationship Development Project" at George Washington University was established to investigate the importance of such transactional processes in mate selection and early marriage. A pilot sample, consisting of 16 premarital couples, who considered themselves to be "seriously attached" and/or engaged, was recruited through advertisements in local newspapers. The couples' length of relationship averaged 2.6 ± 2.3 years; mean age (years) and mean education (years) equalled 25.3 ± 4.1 and 15.1 ± 2.0, for men, and 25.2 ± 5.3 and 16.2 ± 1.8, for women. Four individuals had been married previously, twelve were currently students.

During a semi-structured interview, couples were asked questions designed to tap into each person's family myth and the positions they have taken vis-à-vis these myths (Sample questions: "What are the most important similarities and differences between the families you each came from?"; "What aspect of your family's way of being would you most want to carry into your future? . . . most eagerly change?"; "Given the family that you have come from, can you see any reason why your partner is a particularly good choice for you?"). Almost without exception, these young couples have been able to coherently describe the interdigitation within their relationship of their family of origin experiences in an articulate and emotionally rich manner that suggests a familiarity grounded in prior discussions. Not infrequently, they acknowledge that discussions of each other's families occurred during their first few dates and were important early bonding experiences. The complete protocol for the semi-structured interviews is reproduced in the Appendix.

Three differing postures taken by these young adults vis-à-vis their family myths have emerged from our preliminary, impressionistic analysis. We have called these postures *Accept and Continue, Process and Struggle*, and *Disengage and Repudiate*.

Before describing these postures, two caveats must be mentioned. First, the sampling technique that brought these couples to our laboratory was not designed to generate a random population sample. Therefore, we do not know the frequency of these three postures. While we can state that they are postures that exist — they may be common, they may be rare. Secondly, and more importantly, these postures emerged from analysis of verbal self-report data. Accordingly, they are based on the young adults' conscious conceptions of their relationship and their families of origin. This presents two problems. First, little relationship has been found between self-report of family variables and directly observed family process (Oliveri & Reiss, 1984; Sigafoos, Reiss, Rich & Douglas, 1985). Secondly, prior writing in this area (e.g., Borke, 1967; Dicks, 1967; Napier, 1971) has typically stressed that what these couples would not be able to report, namely, any unconscious themes and processes embedded within their family myths, may be just as, if not more, important than what they did report — this, of course, is a question that we will in time have the data to answer. Still most likely some individuals do unconsciously and *passively perpetuate* their past family reality, and our interview will not identify such a group.

Accept and Continue

Some individuals seem to come from families whose reality has functioned smoothly. Only on rare occasions have they experienced discoveries that run counter to their family's reality. Accordingly, they are able to *accept and continue* a family myth that is quite similar to the reality of their family of origin. We propose that this reported acceptance of the family of origin reflects a deep, personal incorporation of family's reality with the individual's family myth. Typically, their description of their families is full of pride and praise — these young adults often pointed out "unusual" facts about their families, such as their comfort going to their parents for advice or emotional support, their lack of need for teen-age rebellion, that their parents have never divorced, or even more "surprising," that their parents still seem deeply in love. Their descriptions bring to mind the "optimal" families from the Timberlawn study (Lewis, Beavers, Gossett & Phillips, 1976). Although they may express some wishes that some of the individuals in their family would have been different, they find little or no fault with the family as a whole.

> About the only thing that I can think of that I would do differently is that my mom's emphasis on her career has sometimes gone — and she admits this herself — further than she really wants it to — it runs away with her — so that there were periods of time when she wasn't really paying enough attention to things at home or in the family. Dad always filled in and I remember not minding at all helping out because mom really was much happier when she wasn't at home all the time . . . but I was very frustrated when she wasn't home when she said she would be . . . that's something I want to change in our relationship. If I make a promise to Bill or my kids, I'm going to keep it!

Although such lack of turmoil across generations quite frequently raises clinicians' eyebrows in suspicion, the Offers' (1975) research documenting the high frequency of teen-agers who do not evidence tumultuous adolescence and Riskin's (1982) pilot finding that a lack of overt clashes with one's parents is not necessarily detrimental to the task of establishing mature autonomy and independence, support our conjecture that this posture does not automatically indicate latent disturbance.

Process and Struggle

Some individuals enter relationships in a more intermediate position of disengagement from their origin family's reality. While by and large their family of origin reality appears to have served them well, these individuals feel compelled to *process* or *struggle* with some salient family-level relationship issues that have never been satisfactorily resolved within the origin family. They have little problem stating what they liked about their family experience, but as opposed to the first group, these individuals can describe with equal ease areas of their *family's* functioning that they see as fundamentally flawed and in need of repair. Not infrequently their complaints center around the strictness (or lack) of family rules or parental control, the emotional unavailability (or intrusiveness) of other family members, or the tension/conflict that existed in their parents' relationship. The family myth brought into the new relationship is often complex and ambivalently held.

> There is something about his family that I was very attracted to but then I got really sad because our family lacked it. Mom and dad never, well rarely, hugged us or just like kissed us for no reason and we never said, "I love you" in our family. They always say it, they still say it, a lot! . . . I was so sad when I went to the beach with their family for a week. I almost was like, "Get me out of here" because I wished we had that. We had the affection expressed in other ways. A lot of time it was hitting each other—physical things, but never a hug or a kiss or an "I love you"—a slap, a hit would be the most you would ever get.

One is left with the overall impression some domains of family functioning were done "well enough," while others were found lacking.

It is this posture that seems to fit best with the clinical reality of our psychotherapy practices. Not surprisingly, others have discussed similar topics. Borke (1967) studied 25 individuals within two three-generation families, linked through marriage. She concluded that the selection of a marital partner frequently appears to have resulted at least in part from a conscious decision to do something different from what was done in the previous generation, although she proposes that unconscious factors may predominate. Napier (1971), reporting on indepth interviews of two young married couples and all of their parents, concluded that although the couples and their families of origin were more similar than different in their "basic attitude" and psychological make-up, clear evidence existed for cross-generational complementarity on salient relationship issues. Members of each couple on some level felt that some significant, recurrent, interpersonal encounter has been inadequately handled within their family of origin. He further proposed that the exquisitely precise, and frequently unconscious, pairing of individuals on salient relationship issues represented an attempt "to *integrate* disparate elements in the family of origin and to *make overt* what was covert in the original family" (p. 390). To summarize in our terminology, both authors suggest that mate selection is grounded to some extent in the family myths that each person brings into the relationship. Napier goes one step further, proposing that through the selection of a partner with a complementary myth, a situation likely to cause conflict is set up within the new couple as a way to jointly attempt solution of the unsolved problems in each person's family myth.

Disengage and Repudiate

Some individuals frankly describe their family of origin's reality as severely inadequate, even as a failure. Although at some point in time they may have attempted to press for revision of their family's reality, they now appear determined to jump ship to a new family/group and are using their choice of a marital partner to do so. Severe family tension/conflict and the family's failure to adequately handle basic instrumental and/or affectional needs of its members often are described.

> I'd be hard pressed to find anything that I would bring forward or replicate. It serves more to me as a negative role model. Well, I guess I did get left on my own a lot, so now I cherish my peace and quiet, my independence, but I never had a family when that was what I wanted. . . . When I told my parents about my engagement, their reaction was, from my mother, "I'm sorry I can't even wish you good luck," from my father, "A man should be older and more established before he gets married." Hell, I was 28 and making 45K a year! I confronted them at the time as opposed to letting that go as another crock of shit. They really had no response but to follow up on their statements with other supportive arguments of that particular perspective. I've seen them one day since and that's been more than adequate.

The clinical implications of this posture are less clear than for the previous group. While Bowen (1981) has discussed potential risks associated with such "emotional cutoff" from one's heritage, Bennett et al.'s (1987) study of the transmission of alcoholism across generations has shown that the *deliberate* choice of a spouse with a nonalcoholic heritage, combined with subsequent *low contact* with the alcoholic family of origin, is a not uncommon strategy successfully employed by individuals with a strong family history of alcoholism to avoid the reemergence of the illness in their new family. The key seems to be disengaging in a selective manner; the specifics of this process clearly warrant further research. All considered, it seems wise to consider this a high risk move — in jumping ships an individual may not only fall into the water, he/she also may not discover all that lurks in the hold of the partner's ship until they are well into open seas. Nonetheless, for some, these risks may be worth running.

RISKS IN CREATING A REALITY

So far we have focused on the relationship between an individual's family myth and their family reality. We will end with a discussion of how these myths can be patterned within couples. In this paper, we focus on the consequences of selection for the developing relationship, and only briefly discuss the mate selection process. Essentially, the qualitative data we have collected from the couples within the pilot sample suggest that at times a partner is selected who has a similar family myth, at times a partner with different family myth is selected. With time we hope to say more about this process. At this time, our preliminary conclusions seem consistent with those drawn by White and Hatcher (1984) in their recent review of the roles of interpersonal similarity, complementarity and difference in intimate relationships.

On the functional side, given the importance that jointly constructing a new reality has for the successful development of the new family, it seems likely that not all marriages are created equal. Based on the posture taken vis-à-vis their origin family, individuals' family myths are expected to vary in their usefulness in serving as a model for the new reality being constructed. Accordingly, we hypothesize that couples composed of different combinations of the individual postures described above will evidence differences in later marital success/failure. Furthermore, and perhaps more clinically useful, these different combinations are hypothesized to run qualitatively different risks and hence to evidence discernibly different interactional patterns.

We give the best prognosis to those couples made up of individuals who are both *accepting and continuing* their families' realities. The mate selection here is based on similarity. Obviously, this stance frequently goes well with each origin family. Perhaps more surprisingly, couples in our research who appear to evidence such a posture not infrequently describe the ease with which they were accepted into their *in-laws* family.

> I felt incredibly at ease the first time I went over to their house for dinner. It was just like being at my house — everyone dropped whatever they were doing to sit down together for dinner — the talk was loud and furious and went on for hours. Her dad even dominated the conversation just like my dad usually does. I had a nice, warm feeling being there.

The rich connections that they jointly have with their origin families seem likely to serve as potent, twofold, resources. First, the members of the origin families are likely to be available to lend a helping hand when required. Second, and at least as important, their family myths provide detailed, previously successful models of how to make a family work. Accordingly, they have a healthy head start in forming their new reality. We are impressed by the strengths that such couples enter marriage with and are hard pressed to envision what types of problems they might later encounter.

Next best prognosis goes to those couples who are both *processing and struggling* with salient unsolved problems within their family myths. Early marriage for such couples is an exciting "crisis," as they attempt to jointly work out the interpersonal glitches from their past families. There is quite a continuum here, with one pole quite healthy, and the other much less so, based on the extent that the couple's family myths are projected. The central difference between the two extreme types is the ability of the members of the couple to adopt a "systemic" perspective during the conflicts that arise as they jointly wrestle with their interlocked unsolved problems. Some couples are more willing to share the blame or at least hear each other out, while others steadfastly maintain their own innocence, close off channels for potential problem-solving communication, and enter therapy in search of a judicial decision concerning whose myth is best. Dicks (1967) in his classic object relations formulation of marital distress, succinctly describes the central, problematic dynamic that these couples typically encounter, namely, that the complementary attribute in the partner's personality that originally was the major source of attraction, ultimately sours into that person's major vice, when the promise of that attribute dies as the hoped for results repeatedly fail to materialize. For example, with time the rock solid, stable fellow can corrode into the boring, unresponsive obsessive, while the enlivening, light-hearted woman implodes into the dimwitted, flighty hysteric. The goal of therapy, in more family systems terms, requires that each person discovers that the continued power of their own family myth is at least as responsible for the souring of their partner as their partner's actions themselves. The therapist can accomplish this by steadfastly maintaining that *two equal family myths still exist*. The "linear" blames that the couple offers, simply will not do. Instead, a more "circular" explanation, grounded in their family myths and explaining their "crazy" behavior, is required. In our experience, this deceptively simple strategy of conducting the interview with a firm appreciation of the relativity of their individual family myths, frequently is sufficient to allow the transaction construction of their new family reality to continue.

Although John and Roberta had lived together for six years and had a two-year-old daughter, they had not yet married when they presented for therapy. John complained that he "wised up too late" to the fact that Roberta's exciting, fast-paced lifestyle is nothing but "dumb, wasted energy . . . when things get tough, I don't really feel like I can count on her." Similarly, Roberta "now saw" that the solidity and stability that initially attracted her to John, was "due to the fact that he's a prematurely old fart who runs away from strong feelings." Fortunately, they also were willing and able to process how their family myths contributed to their partner's "character pathology."

For each of them, marriage would have been a move of disloyalty. The "good folks" in John's family stayed on the "safe side of the fence." The two he could remember who "crossed over" met "disaster" — Uncle Jeff, a "fun-loving guy" with a penchant for "fast cars and women" was murdered; Cousin Jackie, the "total free spirit" was lost to drugs and prostitution. Still, John acknowledged a fascination with Uncle Jeff — this uncle had always come to his athletic events, while his "overly authoritative" parents never did. Entering therapy, John was convinced that if he married Roberta he would "cross over and seal my fate," since he had left his marriage to his high school sweetheart and four kids to live with Roberta. He was "just playing on the fence" at this time.

Roberta had the opposite problem. Her father was a high-rolling, entrepreneur, whose "bullish practices," although overall quite successful, not infrequently, lead to great fluctuations in family finances and lifestyle. Mother was a "homebody," who constantly complained that she was "stuck" with a husband who loved the stock market more than her and frequently counseled Roberta how to avoid the "mistakes" she made. The essence of mother's message was "don't ever let yourself get tied down." With a successful career and numerous past romantic encounters under her belt, Roberta had taken both father's example and mother's admonition to heart. Unfortunately it was not at all obvious where marriage could fit into her myth.

Once their respective disloyalties were acknowledged, they were able to jointly reinitiate their construction of a new family reality.

Individuals, who are *disengaging from and repudiating* their family myth can do so in two ways. One is to pair with a *rescuer*, i.e., someone who is either *accepting and continuing* or *processing and struggling*, and who accordingly can offer a model of another way to be as a family. The other is to join forces with another person *disengaging from and repudiating* their past to jointly attempt to forge a *new beginning*.

We hypothesize that those *repudiators* who pair with a *rescuer* have a somewhat better prognosis than those who pair with a comparable *new beginner*, although both run relatively high risk. As we mentioned above some of those who jump to a rescuer's ship have made a deal with the devil. These individuals often accept a position of apparent lower power/status in their new family, in return for the "gift" of having some of their instrumental and affectional needs met. This happens most frequently when the rescuer has especially high status with his/her origin family. Problems can arise when the repudiator feels a compelling urgency to change some dimension of the new family's reality and is stymied.

Helen and Mark had been married only 18 months, yet came in for therapy, with a marriage already in considerable trouble. The manifest problem was Helen's drinking. Since their first few dates, Helen had high hopes for her relationship with Mark, having grown up in a small, rather cold, family, who now lived far away. Her mother had died when she was six, and that loss weighed heavily on Helen. She eyed Mark's tightly knit family with awe and envy; she expected that with marriage she would be welcomed with open arms into full family membership. While Mark never promised that, by no means did he ever dissuade her. As the oldest son, Mark was held in highest status, frequently being summoned back to his family's home to handle urgent family matters. All holidays organized first around Mark's family, with Helen typically being informed of finalized plans seemingly as an afterthought.

At first, Helen complied with this arrangement rather dutifully. She had a powerful longing to be part of a good family. With time though her disappointment, resentment, and rage at being a second class citizen grew. There was just no place for her and no need for her opinion in the life of Mark or his family. Mark knew almost everything, and what he didn't his mother or sister did. Through her drinking Helen could on occasion bring all of that to a halt. Once, she was too drunk for Mark to attend his family's reunion; she would have been an unsightly display if he brought her, he would have been embarrassed to attend without her. Further, when drunk she could tell Mark point blank what she thought of his meddling sister; an unpardonable insult if she had been sober. So, although she lacked status in this family system, her drinking captured her some power.

In marital therapy we focused on the degree of imbalance in how their origin family myths were contributing to their new family reality—Helen had lost not only the dream family she had hoped to adopt, but also her origin family myth as well. They were encouraged to begin, perhaps for the first time, to form a new family that they could share.

Of course, sometimes the savior's origin family can accommodate the new member much more easily—not infrequently with the rescuer "donating" his/her place in the family to the partner in a manner so that everyone is happy. Often, the rescuer was a quite rebellious member of his/her origin family—viewed with a systemic lens, the new partner can frequently be a valuable ally for the rescuer in terms of any revisions he or she may be attempting to make within his/her origin family.

For the *new beginning* couples a much more insidious problem can arise, namely, that they drift without a model for relationship success. The family myths that these individuals bring into their relationship allow them to articulate with pointed clarity *what they do not want* to have happen in their new family, but they have a much more difficult time stating *how they want things to be*. Not infrequently, they both   have serious misgivings about marriage as an institution, e.g., "Why do we need a license? It won't help us if things go wrong!" and about having children, "The last thing a child would need is to have a mother like me." It is in this lack of family focus that we believe this group's major weakness lies, since their hesitancy to build significant relational investments as a couple, results in a lack of constraining influences to bind them together during difficult emotional times. Nonetheless, these couples rarely present for conjoint therapy. Rather, they typically present for individual treatment after their latest breakup with a complaint of longstanding difficulty maintaining intimate relationships. We have successfully invited such individuals to return to therapy when they begin their next relationship so as to help them learn (in a rather psychoeducational fashion) how to begin construction of a new, more acceptable, reality.

CONCLUSION

We have presented a process-oriented model of intergenerational family influence, that involves three major constructs: family reality, family myth, and interpersonal transaction. A family's reality is the group-level explanation, that arises out of transaction and coordinates and sustains the interaction of family members. A family myth is an individual-level construction, an internalized schema of the family reality, personalized by the nonfamily transactions experienced by the individual, that an individual takes with him/her as he/she journeys from his/her origin family into the larger world. Each individual entering a serious intimate relationship will have assumed an evaluative posture vis-à-vis his or her family myth. Both jointly attempt to continue and/or rework their family myths by pairing with a partner whose family myth dovetails with their own posture. Once paired, the new couple begins through transaction to integrate their two family myths into a new, hopefully improved, family reality.

Marital and family therapists will benefit in two important ways by focusing on how their clinical couples negotiated this important developmental phase. First, a central point stressed by our research and clinical data is that both individuals' family myths are equally valid. Discussions that proceed from this stance can help shift their conception of what is disturbed in their relationship towards the "nobler" theme of loyalty to one's family myth. Secondly, as they discuss each other's family myths, they invariably mention what they found most dear and most horrid in their origin families. As they do, they frequently voice their hopes, dreams, and aspirations for their marriage. With a mixture of good fortune and skillful handling by their therapist, they may have a transactional experience that they can hold onto and from which they can build into their reality.

REFERENCES

Bateson, G. (1972) *Steps to an ecology of mind*. New York: Ballantine.

Bennett, L.A., Wolin, S.J. & McAvity, K.J. (in press) Family identity, ritual and myth: A cultural perspective on life cycle transitions. In Falicov, K. (Ed.) *Family Transitions*. New York: Guilford.

Bennett, L.A., Wolin, S.J., Reiss, D. & Teitelbaum, M. (1987) Couples at risk for the transmission of alcoholism: Protective influences. *Family Process, 26*, 111-129.

Berger, P.L. & Kellner, H. (1964) Marriage and the construction of reality: An exercise in the microsociology of knowledge. *Diogenes, 46*, 1-24.

Berger, P.L. & Luckmann, T. (1966) *The social construction of reality*. New York: Doubleday.

Borke, H. (1967) A family over three generations: The transmission of interacting and relating patterns. *Journal of Marriage and the Family, 29*, 638-655.

Bowen, M. (1978) *Family therapy in clinical practice*. New York: Jason Aronson.

Byng-Hall, J. (1982) Family legends: Their significance for the family therapist. In A. Bentovim, G.G. Barnes & A. Cooklin (Eds.) *Family therapy: Complementary frameworks of theory and practice, Vol. 1*. New York: Grune & Stratton.

Cooley, C.H. (1909) *Social organization*. New York: Charles Scribner's Sons.

Coyne, J.C. (1985) Toward a theory of frames and reframing: The social nature of frames. *Journal of Marital and Family Therapy, 11*, 337-344.

Dewey, J. & Bentley, A. (1949) *Knowing and the known*. Boston: Beacon Press.

Dicks, H.V. (1967) *Marital tensions*. New York: Basic Books.

Kuhn, T. (1970) *The structure of scientific revolutions, 2nd Ed*. Chicago: University of Chicago Press.

Lewis, J., Beavers, W.R., Gossett, J.T. & Phillips, V.A. (1976) *No single thread: Psychological health in family systems*. New York: Brunner/Mazel.

Marcel, G. (1956) *The philosophy of existentialism*. Secaucus, NJ: Citadel Press.

Mead, G.H. (1934) *Mind, self and society*. Chicago: University of Chicago Press.

Napier, A.Y. (1971) The marriage of families: Cross-generational complementarity. *Family Process, 10*, 373-395.

Offer, D. & Offer, J.B. (1975) *From teenage to young manhood: A psychological study*. New York: Basic Books.

Oliveri, M.E. & Reiss, D. (1981) A theory-based empirical classification of family problem-solving behavior. *Family Process, 20*, 409-418.

Oliveri, M.E. & Reiss, D. (1984) Family concepts and their measurement: Things are seldom what they seem. *Family Process, 23*, 33-48.

Reiss, D. (1981) *The Family's Construction of Reality*. Cambridge, MA: Harvard University Press.

Reiss, D. & Klein, D. (1987) Paradigm and pathogenesis: A family-centered approach to problems of etiology and treatment of psychiatric disorders. In T.

Jacob (Ed.) *Family interaction and psychopathology Theories, methods and findings*. New York: Plenum Press.

Riskin, J. (1982) Research on "nonlabeled" families: A longitudinal study. In F. Walsch (Ed.) *Normal family process*. New York: Guilford Press.

Selvini-Palazzoli, M.S., Boscolo, L., Cecchin, G. & Prata, G. (1978) *Paradox and Counterparadox*. New York: Jason Aronson.

Sigafoos, A., Reiss, D., Rich, J. & Douglas, E. (1985) Pragmatics in the measurement of family functioning: An interpretive framework for methodology. *Family Process, 24*, 189-203.

Steinglass, P., Bennett, L.A., Wolin, S.J. & Reiss, D. (1987) *The Alcoholic Family*. New York: Basic Books.

Stryker, S. (1980) *Symbolic Interactionism*. Menlo Park, CA: Benjamin/Cummings.

Sullivan, H.S. (1953). *The interpersonal theory of psychiatry*. New York: Norton.

Watzlawick, P., Weakland, J. & Fisch, R. (1974) *Change: Principles of problem formation and resolution*. New York: Norton.

White, S.G. & Hatcher, C. (1984) Couple complementarity and similarity: A review of the literature. *American Journal of Family Therapy, 12*, 15-25.

Wolin, S.J. & Bennett, L.A. (1984) Family rituals. *Family Process, 23*, 401-420.

Wolin, S.J., Bennett, L.A., Noonan, D.L. & Teitelbaum, M. (1980) Disrupted family rituals: A factor in the intergenerational transmission of alcoholism. *Journal of Studies in Alcoholism, 41*, 199-214.

APPENDIX

Protocol for Semi-Structured Couples Interviews

Couple's Study Interview Instructions (45 minutes) — This interview is intended to be quite structured — the following questions should all be asked in essentially the same order and wording as stated below. Follow-up questions should be used to obtain clarification/elaboration of vague or unclear responses. Responses must be obtained for all the questions.

1. *Brief Description of Their Relationship* (15 minutes) "It helps me most to begin if you could give me a sketch of your relationship — how you met, some of the things you've been through together, where your relationship is currently at?" Essential points to cover:

—How did they meet?

—Where is their relationship currently at?

—Important challenges so far in their relationship? "As you know all relationships come up against challenges that they have to negotiate—can you tell me about some of the important challenges that you two have successfully made it through?"

2. *The influence of their family backgrounds* (20 minutes) "Now we are going to switch gears and talk about the families you each grew up in."

—Relevant similarities/differences

—What would they most want to conserve?

—What would they most want to change?

—Given the family they grew up in, do they see any reason that their partner is a particularly good or meaningful choice?

—Is their partner ever too much that way? What is that like?

3. *Reaction of their parents to their relationship* (10 minutes) "What do your parents think about your relationship?" or "How have your parents reacted to your being together?"

4. *"Is there anything that I haven't asked that you think is important?"*

Personal, Conjugal and Family Myths: Theoretical, Empirical and Clinical Developments

Dennis A. Bagarozzi
Stephen A. Anderson

SUMMARY. This paper presents the authors' theoretical formulations regarding the development, maintenance and evolution of personal, conjugal and family myths. In addition, several methods for assessing mythological themes are presented. These include the use of empirically derived instruments, structured assessment interviews and behavioral indicators. Several intervention strategies for editing mythological themes also are presented.

We have been using the "myth" concept in our clinical work with individuals, couples, families and primary groups for over a decade now. The first attempt to translate our clinical work (which is guided predominantly by right brain activity) into a language that would allow us to communicate our understanding to other professionals (essentially a left brain activity) resulted in two related papers (Anderson & Bagarozzi, 1983; Bagarozzi & Anderson, 1982). We know that any attempt to communicate something that is essentially intuitive, experiential and analogical via channels that are predominantly logical, digital and intellectual will fall far short of the mark. Keeping this in mind, we would like to offer the reader, who

Dennis A. Bagarozzi, PhD, is in Private Practice at the Alliance for Counseling and Therapeutic Services (ACTS), 42 Lenox Pointe, Atlanta, GA 30324. Stephen A. Anderson, PhD, is Director of the Marital and Family Therapy Training Program and Associate Professor at the University of Connecticut, School of Family Studies, U-117, 843 Bolton Road, Storrs, CT 06268.

is not familiar with our work, a brief review and summary of the major concepts, constructs, axioms and propositions that make up our theoretical system.

First, let us begin with these two axiomatic statements:

1. All myths (whether they be personal, conjugal, familial, group, societal or universal) operate at two interrelated levels of awareness: conscious and unconscious.
2. Family myths are composed of three distinct, yet intimately associated components and processes. These are:
   a. The personal myths of each spouse which are usually comprised of a number of intergenerational themes.
   b. Conjugal myths which crystallize out of the confluence between and among the separate personal themes of both spouses. This process begins during dating and courtship.
   c. Family themes which grow out of the integration of all family members' personal myths, the conjugal themes and myths developed by the spouses and the experiences that are shared by all family members as a group.

THE DEVELOPMENT OF A PERSONAL MYTHOLOGY

Personal mythologies are complexes of symbolic and affectively laden themes consisting of three basic components: the self, the self-in-relation to significant others and internalized cognitive ideals of significant others.

The self, as we conceptualize it, is a superordinate intrapersonal structural system having cognitive and affective components which operate at both conscious and unconscious levels of awareness. The self's primary function is to organize one's experience (both conscious and unconscious) into some coherent whole. The self attempts to bring order and meaning to one's life and one's existence. One's personal behavior and the behaviors of others are perceived, experienced, interpreted and responded to according to how these experiences are subjectively organized and perceived by the self.

One's interpersonal styles evolve as one confronts and attempts to master the various developmental tasks and interpersonal conflicts that occur during each critical stage of the life cycle. The more difficulty an individual has in mastering a particular developmental task, the more this unresolved task will persist as a motif throughout one's life. Such unresolved developmental conflicts continue to resurface as major themes regarding one's *self-in-relation to significant others*.

Early in our work, we made an important observation that later became a fundamental aspect of our clinical approach. Individuals symbolically reflect their unresolved developmental conflicts in their selection of specific fairy tales, folk stories, nursery rhymes, novels, short stories, motion pictures, television programs, etc. These become woven into the themes of their personal mythology. These stories are chosen by the person because they suggest real or symbolic solutions to personal conflicts. Secondly, interventions at the level of fairy tale, story etc., which edit main story lines or the roles of central characters in a person's favorite stories also have the potential to effect the emotional themes and unresolved conflicts these stories have come to symbolically represent.

As we develop in our families of origin, significant persons with whom we come in contact become associated symbolically with specific characters in these fairy tales, stories, etc. through the processes of displacement, projection, transference and object splitting. We also identify with characters in these stories through modeling, introjection and projective identification.

It is important to understand that the significant others themselves also take the form of and are represented to the self as cognitive structures. For example, when one thinks about (consciously or unconsciously) his/her parents, siblings, grandparents, or others and his/her relationships with these individuals, what he/she actually remembers is a reconstruction of events and experiences with *idealized* versions of these persons. Truth or accuracy have little to do with how these persons and one's relationships with them are perceived and/or recalled. Similarly, these reconstructed relationships between and among significant others also become the models for conjugal and familial role expectations and relationship themes.

Environmental experiences and other persons often serve as stimulus cues to an individual which may activate a particular personal theme. In other instances, a person may seek out situations and/or other individuals who unconsciously collude to enact complementary role patterns and thematic dramas. This process allows the person to enter into what appears to be new and different relationships which, nevertheless, have familiar patterns and predictable outcomes. We view this repetitive, almost ritualistic, process as involving elements of transference and projective identification and as an attempt to rework and correct unresolved conflicts.

The family of origin and the relationship dynamics that occur therein can be considered to constitute a rough blueprint for the development of central themes in one's personal mythology.

Personal myths also can be viewed as serving the function of explaining and guiding human behavior in a manner analogous to the role played by cultural myths in all societies. They give meaning to the past, establish continuity, define the present and provide direction for the future (Feinstein, 1979). Personal myths allow us to organize our experiences in a way that gives them some psychological meaning and significance.

THE ROLE OF COGNITIVE IDEALS IN THE DEVELOPMENT OF CONJUGAL THEMES AND THE EVOLUTION OF CONJUGAL MYTHS

As a result of experience with significant members of the opposite sex and from repeated exposure to familial models and other important male/female relationships, one develops cognitive representations of his/her *ideal spouse* and his/her *ideal marriage*. These *ideals* have both conscious and unconscious elements and serve as standards against which all prospective mates and marriages are judged and evaluated. It is assumed that persons actively seek out and marry individuals whom they believe will behave in accordance with these internalized cognitive *ideals*. In previous papers, we have referred to this search for the ideal as "cognitive matching" (Bagarozzi, 1982, 1986; Bagarozzi & Giddings, 1983, 1984).

The *ideal spouse*-in-relation-to-the-*self* in the context of one's *ideal marriage* becomes a central theme when one is preparing for marriage and actively seeking a mate. Prospective spouses are chosen because they are perceived as being able to "fit" into important themes in the individual's personal mythology. The meshing of both individuals' personal themes and myths that takes place during the courtship process is the logical link between individual dynamics and marital dynamics. This coming together of themes from two personal mythologies becomes the foundation for the development of a unique conjugal mythology. Conjugal mythology is the concept we use to describe this loosely organized complex of spouses' personal themes that stand in various types of relationships to each other.

Throughout the courtship process, intrapersonal and dyadic equilibria are simultaneously maintained so long as the prospective mate's behavior is perceived to be in accordance with one's *ideal*. However, when one's prospective mate's behavior deviates too drastically from the *ideal*, disequilibrium results. Such disequilibrium can be corrected in several ways: (a) one recognizes the discrepancy and terminates the relationship, (b) one modifies his/her *ideal* (through assimilation and accommodation) so that it becomes more consistent with reality, or (c) one denies that any discrepancy exists but waits until after marriage before he/she attempts to alter or change his/her spouse so that he/she conforms more closely to this ideal.

One's *ideal spouse* is thought to possess certain desirable qualities, traits, and behavioral characteristics (e.g., personal autonomy, courage, intelligence etc.) and to share a similar level of individuation from the family of origin. In addition, the ideal spouse is expected to share (with his/her prospective mate) the same relationship rules in certain critical areas of marriage. These include, rules for intimacy (closeness and separateness), distributive justice and social exchange, sharing power and influence, and rules for sending and receiving messages that convey esteem and value for one's spouse.

Marital conflicts inevitably develop whenever spouses begin to realize the discrepancies between their *ideal* and *perceived* mates in any of these domains, and attempt to bring about behavioral and characterological changes through coercion, punishment and negative reinforcements. These attempts by both spouses to subtly (or not so subtly) coerce their mates into behaving and becoming more like their ideals has been termed "mutual shaping toward the ideal" (Bagarozzi & Giddings, 1983, 1984). In order to arrive at a successful resolution of these conflicts and differences, spouses must learn how to reach mutually agreed upon solutions in those areas where there are perceived/ideal discrepancies, relationship rules are grossly different and value messages are discrepant. Unfortunately, all discrepancies and differences are not consciously recognized and openly negotiated in marriage, and couples often enter into unconscious contracts (Sager, 1976) and collusive agreements (Dicks, 1967) which are designed to end the conflict and protect both spouses. These unconscious contracts and collusive arrangements are incorporated into the couple's developing conjugal mythology.

There are several additional dynamics, in the mate selection process, that play a part in the development and maintenance of marital conflicts in distressed relationships. These include:

1. Spouses are chosen because both individuals perceive their prospective mates as possessing certain traits, qualities, characteristics, etc. that he/she lacks and desires to obtain through intimate association (e.g., confidence, competence, self-esteem) with his/her spouse-to-be.

2. Both spouses select mates who represent central characters in their personal mythologies with whom they have a number of unresolved conflicts. By choosing such a spouse, each person attempts to recreate central conflicts and themes in his/her marriage with the hope of successfully resolving them through transference acting out.

3. Although the *ideal spouse* usually is composed of predominantly positive traits and characteristics, he/she does not represent perfection. Negative qualities are also part of one's *ideal*. However, in more distressed marriages, projective identification becomes a central mechanism used by both spouses to deal with the inevitable disappointments that occur when one confronts gross discrepancies between one's *ideal* and perceived mate. In the process, each spouse represses, denies and projects his/her own unacceptable, negative traits, wishes, desires, beliefs, part objects, etc. onto his/her spouse who then becomes the target of attack and criticism for possessing these undesirable characteristics. Frequently, both spouses unconsciously contract to enact the complementary roles the other spouse requires to rework unresolved conflicts with significant others.

Understanding a person's fantasized relationship with his/her *ideal spouse* is essential if one wishes to learn more about the disappointments that lead to marital conflicts and the myths that couples develop in order to reach some sort of unconscious compromise that permits them to continue in the marriage.

CONJUGAL MYTHS: ASSESSMENT CONSIDERATIONS

We have devoted a considerable amount of time to discussing our methods for assessing personal, conjugal and family myths elsewhere (Bagarozzi & Anderson, in press). Therefore, in this section we will briefly review our methods for assessing couples' conjugal mythologies and then follow this with some clinical material to illustrate the links between our theoretical formulations and assessment methods.

Empirically Derived Instruments

In our attempt to investigate some of the conscious and preconscious dimensions of the *ideal spouse*, we developed IMAGES (Anderson, Bagarozzi & Giddings, 1986). IMAGES is a 35 item, self-report instrument consisting of seven relatively independent subscales empirically established through factor analysis. Each subscale factor has been statistically tested to determine its internal consistency. Cronbach alpha correlations for these subscales range from .70 to .87. The seven subscales assess the following sets of spousal characteristics: Emotional Gratification and Support; Sex Role Orientation and Physical Attraction; Satisfaction with one's spouse in the areas of Sexual, Emotional and Intellectual Intimacy; Parent-Sibling Indentification; Emotional Maturity; Intelligence and Homogamy (similarity along ethnic, cultural, racial, socioeconomic and religious lines).

Each spouse is asked to rate, on a 7 point Likert type scale, the degree to which his/her spouse corresponds to his/her ideal for each of the 35 items. Each spouse is also asked to consider how important each of the 35 behaviorally worded items is in determining his/her satisfaction with his/her chosen mate.

By using IMAGES, we are able to gather direct information about which ideal spouse/perceived spouse discrepancies serve as a source of conflict in the marriage. In order to gain more information concerning spouses' levels of individuation and ideal/perceived discrepancies in the various areas of relationship rules outlined above, we use the following empirical instruments and observational procedures:

1. Individuation: Personal Authority in the Family Systems Questionnaire (Bray, Williamson & Malone, 1984).
2. Closeness and Separateness: FACES III: Family Adaptability and Cohesion Scale (Olson, Portner & Lavee, 1985).
3. Distributive Justice and Social Exchange: SIDCARB: Spousal Inventory of Desired Changes and Relationship Barriers (Bagarozzi, 1983).
4. Sharing Power and Influence: Relational Communication Coding System (Rogers and Bagarozzi, 1983).

To assess the fifth dimension, rules for sending and receiving messages that convey esteem and value for one's spouses, we assign any number of conflict negotiation tasks and problem solving exercises to couples so that we can observe their actual behavior, typical interaction styles and characteristic ways of sending and receiving value messages. We also ask each spouse to identify what he/she says and does that he/she believes is perceived by his/her mate as an expression of love, affection, appreciation and valuing. Spouses are also asked to identify what they say and do that they believe their mates experience as devaluing or derogatory.

Initial Assessment Interviews

We have developed a number of structured interviews which we have found valuable both for research and clinical assessment. During the initial assessment, we usually begin by meeting with both spouses and asking detailed questions about the *Couple's Relationship History* (27 questions) and the *History of the Presenting Problem* (17 questions). We view the presenting problem as a condensed, and symbolically rich manifestation of the couple's conjugal mythology. We will often see each spouse individually to ask detailed questions about each spouse's *Family Relationships History* (41 questions) and to conduct *Personal Myth Assessment*

Interviews (14 questions). The *Personal Myth Assessment Interview* is a projective technique to further our understanding of central conflicts and accompanying themes (Bagarozzi & Anderson, in press).

The information obtained from both the empirical instruments and the assessment interviews allows us to understand:

1. How personal themes manifest themselves in each spouse's responses to the assessment instruments.
2. How specific personal themes manifest themselves in the spouses' behavior and communication styles.
3. How the various themes from both spouses' personal mythologies have become woven together to form conjoint themes that constitute the couple's conjugal mythology.

Using Behavioral Indicators to Highlight Couples' Mythological Themes

As noted above, when working with couples, we are especially interested in the meshing of personal themes and mythologies. We are interested in the enduring cognitive appraisals each spouse makes of the partner in relation to their own internalized standards for their ideal spouse and ideal marriage. We pay close attention to the recurring transactional rules couples both report and enact during therapeutic sessions. We also are cognizant of the prominent affects which comprise major portions of the couple's emotional experience. And, we are attuned to the symbolic significance of the presenting problem as a repository for these enduring cognitions, interactional rules and affects. To organize all of this information into a useful understanding of a couple's conjugal mythology, we use the following four indicators: (a) Recurrent topics of concern, (b) Redundancy of interaction patterns, (c) Repeated resurfacing of affect laden conflicts, and (d) The couple's predominant feeling or affective tone. A brief case example is offered here to illustrate the use of these behavioral indicators. Later in this paper we will illustrate how the empirical instruments and structured assessment interviews are used clinically.

Recurrent Topics of Concern. While the presenting problem is often a major topic of concern, other issues may also routinely surface and provide important information about significant themes in a couple's mythology. For instance, a couple recently sought therapy initially for the wife's depression and suicidal ideation. The husband, Mr. M., was at his wit's end, frustrated and fearful he would be unable to continue with the marriage. His time at home alternated between monitoring Mrs. M.'s every move and worrying about her well-being, and angry outbursts of frustration followed by withdrawing from her out of fear that he would explode and hurt her. Her requests for more closeness were perceived by him as impossible as he felt he was already doing everything he could to satisfy and reassure her. For her part, Mrs. M. felt defeated, isolated, misunderstood and rejected by her husband. While the overriding concern of both partners during the initial assessment interviews was Mrs. M.'s depression, several other major recurring concerns were also identified.

Foremost among these was Mrs. M.'s secondary presenting complaint about Mr. M.'s masturbation which varied from once every several weeks to several times a week. While conceding that masturbation was a "normal activity" which she engaged in herself, Mrs. M. perceived her husband's masturbation to be an indication that he thought she was unattractive, undesirable and unimportant to him. Her response to his masturbation was to monitor his behavior in the bathroom, to check his clothes for "evidence" and to aggressively monitor his behavior whenever he was home but out of her sight. These aggressive behaviors were in sharp contrast to Mrs. M.'s depressed, withdrawn and submissive behavior toward her husband in other aspects of their relationship.

Several other recurrent concerns were noted. These included Mrs. M.'s problematic relationship with her mother who was described as intrusive, controlling, dogmatic, selfish and insensitive. The periodic visits by Mrs. M.'s mother were preceded by a week of apprehension and anxiety and followed by another week of frustration, annoyance and regret over lost opportunities to put her "in her place." Mr. M. frequently expressed concerns about his work where he often felt pressed upon to assume more responsibility than he had authority to assume and often felt "cornered" into a "no win" situation of being asked to do more, then being reprimanded for doing it. A final noteworthy concern expressed by both spouses was their strong investment in insuring that the other was not distressed. Whenever one of the couple appeared emotionally upset, the other became activated to worry, console or otherwise offer to make amends. Both dreaded the prospect of separation which arose each time an emotional outburst occurred.

Redundant Interaction Patterns. As noted earlier, the ritualized quality of couple's interactions over time constitute an important element of the couple's conjugal mythology. For Mr. and Mrs. M., the rules regarding managing interpersonal closeness and distance emerged as central. Mrs. M.'s desire for emotional support, closeness and reassurance often involved approaching Mr. M. and asking him how he was feeling. Was he angry at her? Had she done something wrong to upset him? His response was to either deny that he was upset or, if he was upset, to acknowledge it, and then request some "time alone" to work it out. Mr. M.'s distancing when upset further reinforced Mrs. M.'s anxiety, and need for reassurance. However, her response was typically to withdraw, to cry, and to remain aloof. Mr. M.'s typical response to Mrs. M.'s tears and withdrawal was to then become concerned about her depression and suicide potential and to approach her to talk about her condition. These interactions would, at some point, break down with Mr. M. becoming frustrated and angry, feeling that too much was being demanded of him or that he was being reprimanded for not responding appropriately. He would become frightened about "losing control" or desperate over the prospect of the marriage ending, and withdraw to his workshop or some other neutral place to deal with his feelings alone. Mr. M.'s withdrawal would again precipitate Mrs. M's inquisitive, approaching behaviors and the sequence would begin anew.

Repeated Affect-Laden Conflicts. One often finds that conflicts which continue to surface tend to include many of the topics of concern which have been voiced by one or both spouses. These affect laden conflicts tend to resurface with some regularity and have a familiar quality about them. For the couple described above, intense conflicts centered around issues regarding closeness and distance, satisfying the needs of self versus other, negotiating rules for the distribution of power and handling aggression.

Predominant Affective Tone. It has been our experience that in distressed couples, there is a severe restriction in the variety or range of emotions expressed (Anderson & Bagarozzi, 1983; Bagarozzi & Anderson, 1982; Epstein, Bishop & Levin, 1978; Lewis, Beavers, Gossett & Phillips, 1976). This is often a clue to the central themes of the couple's conjugal mythology. In the case previously noted, the predominant tone was one of desperation and fear of loss (loss of spouse, loss of control, loss of self).

When information from the previously mentioned four indicators was combined with information regarding each spouse's personal mythology, we began to formulate an overview of the couple's conjugal mythology. Although the actual exploration of Mr. and Mrs. M.'s personal mythologies was a complex and lengthy process, abbreviated versions are included here for heuristic purposes. In Mrs. M.'s family of origin, her mother was a powerful force to be dealt with. Mrs. M., her father and her two sisters all shared a similar orientation to Mrs. M.'s mother which was to not challenge her when conflicts developed. As a result of this family structure as well as other factors, Mrs. M. had developed a personal mythology which included the following conceptions of self and self in-relation-to others:

> I'm not as important, nor are my needs as important as the needs of others in my life. When disputes arise between my needs and those of significant others, I should withdraw, defer to them and not challenge the status quo. To challenge would mean risking the support of the important people in my life. This would leave me alone, vulnerable and unable to defend myself against powerful others particularly women who have only their own selfish interests at heart.

In Mr. M.'s family of origin, a somewhat disengaged family structure prevailed. Mr. M. and his two brothers were free to come and go as they pleased. His parents had divorced during his school years and his contact with his father was very limited. While living with his mother, whose health was poor, he often had to fend for himself. Conflicts when they arose in this family were generally avoided. Mr. M.'s personal mythology included the following:

> Life is good when I'm in charge. When I can take responsibility without interference, work gets done, I'm more relaxed and I can be more responsive to others. At times, I feel tired and overextended. However, this would not be a problem if others would allow me to function without interference. When unpleasant conflicts arise, I can usually keep others at bay by threatening to unleash my powerful temper. This temper is a force to be reckoned with, as once, I almost killed someone when it erupted. If my threat fails, and because I dread actually using this deadly weapon, I will generally withdraw from others to deal with my feelings and reactions alone. I must always leave myself a way out of interpersonal encounters. Otherwise, I might have to fight, lose control and really hurt someone.

When information from the behavioral indicators and each spouse's personal mythology was reviewed, the following scenario of the couple's conjugal mythology emerged. Mrs. M. felt overpowered and defeated in her relationships with husband in much the same way she had with her mother in her family of origin. In disagreements with either, it was she who "gave in," "sacrificed (her) self" for the sake of the other. Mr. M.'s style of unleashing intense anger, fearing his anger's destructive potential, and then distancing from conflict to deal with it alone, had always been effective and periodically reinforced in both his family of origin and in his marriage. In each area of his life (work, family of origin, marriage) he experienced pressure to take responsibility for the well-being of others and criticism because his efforts were unappreciated. His response was the desire to retreat from this while simultaneously wanting to maintain the interpersonal power and security this role provided.

Mr. and Mrs. M.'s secondary presenting complaint, that of Mr. M.'s masturbation symbolically recreated each spouse's original conflicts from their families of origin in their current marriage. The issue for Mrs. M. was

you'd rather satisfy your own needs than to help me satisfy
mine. When things get tense between us you take things into
your own hands and forget about me. I will not let this happen
to me again. I'll follow you around, monitor your every move
rather than to sacrifice my needs again.

Mr. M.'s part in the script could be read as follows:

you are trying to corner me and make me give up "my self"
and the little freedom in my life that remains. If you keep
pressuring me like this I will explode. I've exploded before
and the consequences were nearly catastrophic as someone almost died. If I lose control, I fear I will be left all alone as you
will not be strong enough to handle my rage and vulnerability.
This relationship is the most important part of my otherwise
empty and disengaged life. Therefore, it is safer for me to
discharge my pressure on my own than to risk losing you.
Leave me alone.

Threaded throughout this couple's conjugal mythology were efforts to reenact personal unresolved themes by collusively arranging
for each spouse to play the reciprocal roles required by the other.
Mrs. M.'s sense of her self as competent, assertive, and deserving
and her need to "correct" past injustices was concentrated in her
intense monitoring of her husband's masturbatory behavior. The
tenacity of Mrs. M.'s efforts was matched by the tenacity with
which Mr. M. refused to relinquish the "safety valve" that protected him from fully losing control, and with that loss of control,
all that he valued in his life.

FAMILY MYTHS AND THEIR EVOLUTION

As we said earlier, family myths are comprised of three interrelated components: (a) the personal myths of each spouse, (b) the
complex of interrelated personal themes of both spouses that make
up the couple's conjugal mythology, and (c) the family group myths
which emerge from the meshing and integration of all family members' personal myths, the conjugal myths of parents and the shared

experiences of all family members as a group. The arrival of the first child can be considered a critical period in the development of the family's mythology. Both spouses have their own conscious and unconscious, "ideal" expectations for each child before it is born and after it enters the family. These expectations can be appropriate or inappropriate, realistic or unrealistic, socially acceptable and adaptive or socially unacceptable, maladaptive or deviant.

In families that fall within the "normal" or "healthy" range of functioning, each parent's consciously held expectations for each child are consistent with his/her unconsciously held expectations for this same child, and both parents share similar, more or less, compatible expectations for the same child.

In more distressed family systems, however, little consistency exists *intrapersonally* (between the conscious and unconscious expectations of one or both parents). Behaviorally, this is evidenced in the ambivalent treatment of the child and in inconsistent, contradictory or double bind messages directed toward the child. Similarly, there is frequently *interpersonal* disagreement (conscious and/or unconscious) between the parents concerning their expectations for the child. The child who becomes the focal point of such parental struggle usually develops a psychiatric symptom as an attempt to deal with these unverbalized and, often, unresolvable conflicts. In doing so, he/she becomes a symbol or metaphor of the unconscious parental struggle.

In dysfunctional family systems, one child usually becomes the focal point of parents' conflicting, conscious and unconscious expectations, with other children and family members performing supporting roles. Some of the most common dysfunctional expectations that parents have for this child include that he/she: (a) fulfill the parent's unmet needs that "should have" been satisfied by that parent's parents (e.g., nurturance, love, protection, admiration), (b) correct all wrongs that the parent experienced in his/her family of origin, (c) augment the parent's self-esteem or provide the parent with self-esteem, (d) achieve what the parent could not achieve or was prevented from achieving by significant others, (e) become an extension of the parent who has no clear identity of his/her own, or who perceives separation-individuation as a threat, or as abandon-

ment, (f) coalign with the parent against his/her spouse in marital
conflicts and power disputes, (g) take the place of one's spouse who
is physically or emotionally unavailable.[1]

Diagnostic Considerations

In our clinical work with families, we use the same battery of
instruments, interviews, assigned behavioral tasks and behavioral
indicators that are used with couples to gain access to the salient
themes that constitute the family's mythological system. We also
have found that family themes tend to cluster around unresolved
developmental issues. For example:

1. Nurturance, trust, separation, loss, abandonment, separate-
   ness-closeness, etc.
2. Autonomy, individuation, mastery, etc.
3. Dominance, submission, competency, competition, coopera-
   tion.
4. Genital sexuality, sex role and gender identity, masculinity
   femininity, etc.
5. Ego identity, pregnancy, childbirth, death, rebirth, etc.

In the initial interview, we attend to the following:

1. *Identify the key roles played by each family member as they contribute to the family maintaining a homeostatic balance and as
   they contribute to the family's ability to grow, develop and remain viable.*

Each family member is encouraged to share his/her perception of
what he/she does that is important for maintaining the family as a
unit and for helping the family grow and change.

2. *Identify any labels that are used to describe any family members.*

Once these have been identified, we trace their origins in order to
determine whether these labels (nicknames, pet names, derogatory
names, epithets, etc.) actually prescribe specific behaviors for that
individual. In addition, we explore the meaning that such labels
have for the labelled individual and all other family members.

3. *Have each family member describe the family in analogical and metaphorical terms.*

For example, what does it mean when a person describes his/her family as being "solid as the Rock of Gibraltar" (analogy)? What does one mean when he/she compares the parents' relationship to their children as "generals to their troops" (metaphor)?

4. *Have each family member describe his/her perceived role relationships with each member of the family and the family as a whole unit in terms of an analogy and a metaphor.*

For example, if the family is as "solid as the Rock of Gibraltar," how are you related to this rock? Are you a pebble? a tree? grass? the ocean? If the father is described as the "Big Bad Wolf," who are the other members of the family? Which family members represent the "Three Little Pigs"? Who is the Hunter who kills the Big Bad Wolf?

5. *Identify those ritualized behaviors of family members that have a "more of the same" quality and attempt to discern the symbolic meaning which ties these behaviors to central family themes.*

By identifying a given ritual and understanding its meaning, we gain valuable information that can be used to edit family myths later in therapy.

We also develop structural descriptions, as suggested by Minuchin (1974), to identify hierarchical arrangements, types of boundaries observed, coalitions, affiliations, over involvements, conflicts or triangles that maintain dysfunctional family structures. Once these have been identified, we attempt to unearth the covert beliefs or sub myths which are used to maintain these structures. For example, a mother-daughter coalition may be maintained by the shared sub myth that "men are dangerous and should never be trusted"; a father-daughter coalition may be maintained by the shared myth that "mother is too fragile and sickly to be told anything unpleasant." Therefore, father and daughter make all the financial decisions in the family.

Families often use what we have termed "the openly acknowledged family myth" as a group defense. For example, a family presents itself for the first interview, and the two teenage children begin to argue. The oldest child, a boy, attacks his sister for being "daddy's little girl," and all family members (including the daughter) agree that she is the father's favorite. The family then proceeds to offer a litany of reasons to legitimize the daughter's exalted status. The family's agreement and its willingness to discuss what seems to be a significant theme or "myth" is used to divert, to confuse and to lead the therapist away from the focal conflicts for which this "myth" is a smoke screen.

The interrelationships between parental expectations for a child, parents' unresolved developmental conflicts, the current symptomatic behavior of a child, the family's present developmental impasse and the family's ritualized behaviors are illustrated in the case of a single-parent mother of a fifteen- and a seventeen-year-old daughter. The mother had been sexually abused by her father when she was a teenager. When, after several years of continued abuse, she had revealed the incidents to her own mother and later to her two brothers, she was met with denial, disbelief and accusations that she was lying. The father also accused her of lying. Her response to her family was to feel betrayed and isolated.

From that time on, the theme of betrayal and isolation continued to recur in this woman's interpersonal experiences. When her mother died unexpectedly in an automobile accident, the woman felt betrayed and isolated because she had never been able to reconnect with her own mother while she was still alive. Several years later, her father was accused by a stepdaughter of sexual abuse. And, even though her brothers now believed that their sister had also been sexually abused, they were unable to support her when, on several occasions, she attempted to confront her father for his actions. Each time her brothers looked the other way, unable to challenge their father. Again, she felt betrayed and isolated.

The theme also dominated her heterosexual relationships. She had been abandoned by her husband shortly after the birth of her second daughter. Prior to beginning therapy, she had become engaged to be married to a man she had been living with for several years. Just following his proposal of marriage, he unexpectedly decided to break off the relationship and had moved out of her home.

The presenting problem in this case was the sexual promiscuity of the younger 15-year-old daughter who had been staying out all night and had recently run away from home. The 17-year-old daughter was about to graduate from high school and had been making plans to move away from home to college.

It is our contention that the youngest daughter's symptomatic behavior can be understood as fulfilling her mother's unconscious expectations, as a reenactment of her mother's own unresolved issues regarding sexuality and as the last in a long series of previously unsuccessful efforts to edit a myth of abandonment and betrayal. The family's need to edit this myth was especially striking at this developmental stage. If the older daughter was to successfully individuate and still maintain a sense of connectedness with her mother, she needed to leave in a context other than abandonment and betrayal since that has resulted in emotional cutoffs in the past. The youngest daughter's actions focused attention away from the oldest daughter's impending departure and offered a new opportunity to edit the myth. In this family, separations, whether they were temporary or permanent, had a symbolic, affectively-laden, ritualistic quality. For the mother, each separation precipitated familiar feelings of depression and concerns that others were never available when they were needed. For both daughters, separations precipitated fearful concern for their mother and frustration, because their efforts to be available to support their mother went unrecognized. Such gestures of support and availability were not a part of the prevailing family myth.

CLINICAL STRATEGIES

We have devoted a considerable amount of time to discussing treatment strategies that we have developed to edit personal, conjugal and family mythologies (Bagarozzi & Anderson, in press), and we cannot attempt to review them all in this brief article. However, we will describe a few of them which we have used in our work with couples and families. The first strategy is one designed to help spouses begin the process of reducing their conscious, ideal spouse/ perceived discrepancies.

Structured Training in Communication. Spouses responses to IMAGES are used to help the couple identify ideal spouse/per-

ceived spouse discrepancies that are major sources of disappointment and conflict. Once these have been identified, spouses are
taught functional communication skills that they can use to discuss
their disappointments, thoughts, feelings, perceptions, attributions,
etc. as they relate to the particular behavioral trait or characteristic
under consideration.

This exercise allows spouses to verbalize and discuss their disappointments concerning ideal spouse/perceived spouse discrepancies
in an atmosphere of mutual trust and respect. In such an atmosphere, modification of one's cognitive ideal is more likely to take
place. Similarly, spouses will be more prone to make changes in
their own behavior if the threat of criticism and blame is removed.
This exercise also lays the groundwork for the use of symbolic behavioral contracts, a strategy used to edit dysfunctional conjugal
themes, later in therapy. These communication exercises also facilitate the development of role taking, empathy, and intimacy between
the spouses.

A similar technique, with some modification, has been developed for families in order to help detriangulate the identified patient
who is caught between two conflicting ideal child images. In this
variation, we first help parents to become aware of their conflicting
and sometimes incompatible role expectations for the identified patient. Once these have been identified, parents are asked to discuss
these differences, their conflicts over these differences, their disappointments, etc. in the presence of the identified patient who is
encouraged to ask his/her parents any questions that he/she would
like them to answer about the issue at hand. At the close of the
discussion, the therapist remarks how the identified patient's symptomatic behavior actually represents the identified patient's attempt
to enact two incompatible, conflicting and contradictory expectations. In essence, the identified patient's symptomatic behavior is
an attempt to please both parents.

Usually, such a revelation forces the parents to come up with a
mutually agreed upon, more realistic set of expectations for the
identified patient, and they are more willing to work, as a team, to
bring the child's symptomatic behavior under control. However,
this may not always be the case, and in severely distressed family

systems, detriangulation of the identified patient may require more indirect intervention strategies which are less threatening.

Rites of Passage. Ancient cultures and primitive societies have developed rites of passage to help individuals move from one stage of the life cycle to the next. We have found such rites of passage especially helpful in families where the identified patient is an adolescent.

Adolescence offers young people, in our contemporary Western society, the developmental task of establishing and consolidating a unique personal identity as well as a second chance to rework and successfully master whatever developmental tasks that remain unresolved from previous developmental eras (Erikson, 1968). The more triangulated the child is between conflicting parental projections and expectations, the more difficult it will be for him/her to establish autonomy in early childhood and to develop a clear, separate identity during adolescence. Adolescents who are trapped in such an impasse will often resort to drastic and desperate measures to separate from their families of origin, to rid themselves of parental projections, to develop their own set of values and moral principles and to consolidate their own unique personal identities. Acting out behavior, substance abuse, sexual promiscuity, psychiatric disturbance or suicidal attempts all can be seen as the adolescent's dramatic attempt to free himself/herself from such an intolerable position which, if allowed to continue, would end in psychic death.

Scholars have identified three stages through which all rites of passage proceed: separation, transition and incorporation (van Gennep, 1960). Initiation ceremonies are predominantly rites of transition which help the initiate progress from one stage of life (childhood) to the next stage (adulthood) in a smooth, orderly and predictable fashion. In primitive societies, initiation usually takes place in same sex groups. During such ritual practices, the initiates are removed from their families of origin. Males are usually subjected to ordeals and trials of endurance by their elders. These trials might include physical beating, hazing, humiliation, homosexual submission and mutilation (e.g., circumcision, subincision, scarring, tattooing, removal of teeth, etc.). In addition, males are instructed in tribal lore, myths, male secrets and traditions. A central theme of male initiation ceremonies is the ritual slaying of the initiatc, his subsequent death and his joyful resurrection as a changed person. All initiation rites take place under the watchful eyes of the elders and tribal gods.

Female initiation rites, though less common in primitive societies, usually consist of the recognition that menstruation has begun and that the young initiate has now begun the reproductive phase of her life. She, too, is taught tribal lore, myths, women's secrets and traditions. Female initiation usually takes place in stages, i.e., dealing with menstruation, pregnancy and childbirth. Female initiations have as their central theme, "the mystery of giving birth." The young woman learns that she is "creative upon the plane of life" (Eliade, 1960; p. 216). This revelation is a religious experience that has no masculine counterpart.

Unfortunately, few organized and culturally prescribed rites of passage exist in Western society which enable the teenager to make a relatively smooth passage into adulthood. In most instances, the adolescent experiences his/her rites of passage via a same sex peer group unsupervised by adults. For males and females attending college, fraternities and sororities come closest to primitive societies in providing the major ingredients associated with tribal rites of passage. The military also serves this function for many men, and now some women. In the first author's work with fighting gangs that roamed the streets of the Southeast Bronx, Harlem and Spanish Harlem during the late 1960s, it was not unusual to find many of the practices characteristic of tribal initiation ceremonies present in the initiate's induction into the gang.

Same sex peer groups, for better or for worse, take the place of the tribal group of elders for the majority of adolescents in our culture. Teenagers who have not had the benefit of forming a close interpersonal "chum" relationship (Sullivan, 1953) with a member of the same sex during preadolescence can recoup their losses, to a large degree, if they can become part of a same sex adolescent peer group.

In our work with families where the identified patient is an adolescent, we frequently find that he/she has been unable to find a peer group that is able to support his/her attempts at separation individuation from his/her family of origin. The more isolated the youngster is from friends his/her own age, the poorer the prognosis.

The peer group is extremely helpful, because it encourages the youngster to divest himself/herself of parental projections and expectations and provides a supportive environment where he/she can try out various roles, experiment with interpersonal relationships and begin the process of identity formation. In such cases, we attempt to design intervention strategies (based upon our understanding of each family member's personal mythology, the parent's conjugal mythology and the family group myth) that simulate rites of passage and facilitate the adolescent's entry into an appropriate peer group.

We do this by helping families develop a number of carefully designed, symbolic, ritual contracts that serve as rites of passage for the identified patient. For example: permitting the identified patient to get a job that will enable him/her to earn spending money, allowing the identified patient to date members of the opposite sex, extending his/her curfew on weekends, permitting the identified patient to use the family car in exchange for improving school grades, or completing chores around the house can be the first step in the emancipation process. As each contract is negotiated, the identified patient is reminded of the increased responsibility that comes with "becoming a man" or "becoming a woman."

Parents are helped to discuss their ambivalence about their child's newfound freedom. At times, we have held sessions with parents on Friday evenings when the identified patient was out on a date or using the family car. During these sessions, we redirect parents to issues in their own relationship, help them negotiate new marital contracts that strengthen the parental coalition and reinforce subsystem boundaries.

Ritual prescriptions that make use of central family themes can be devised to simulate death and rebirth of the identified patient or to celebrate the transition to womanhood for females in the family. Ceremonies where parents give their children treasured heirlooms, personal belongings and reveal family secrets are another way of introducing rites of passage into the family therapy session. Depending upon the family's socio cultural, ethnic and religious background, specific activities can be prescribed that represent initiation rituals into adulthood. For example, fathers can teach their sons how to hunt. fish, drive, play a particular sport, or follow the stock market. Mothers can teach their daughters how to cook, drive, put on make-up, say "no" to boys, or be assertive and compete on equal footing with males.

Role Compromise of Central Characters. Material gathered in the *Personal Myth Assessment Interviews* regarding spouses' and family members' favorite stories, plays a central part in our approach to editing conjugal and family myths. For illustrative purposes, we will use a clinical example to describe one of the many intervention strategies we have developed to disrupt dysfunctional homeostatic cycles in marital therapy.

Mr. and Mrs. Brown came in for marital therapy with two presenting problems: "a power struggle" and "poor communication." This struggle permeated their marital relationship to the point where the couple would openly argue in supermarkets about what types of groceries to buy. Conflicts over closeness and separateness were evident in FACES III scores, Mr. Brown pressed for more closeness and Mrs. Brown wanted more separateness. Both spouses had successfully separated and individuated from their families of origin. This was evident by their responses to PAFS. In addition, both Mr. and Mrs. Brown possessed about equal power in the marriage as evidenced by their SIDCARB scores. Both had valuable resources that were prized by the other and neither spouse perceived serious barriers to separation or divorce. As far as both were concerned, the marriage was completely voluntary. This balance of power had led to a stalemate. Both Mr. and Mrs. Brown recorded major perceived spouse/ideal spouse discrepancies as measured by IMAGES. These differences had existed for 24 years, but only became a "serious problem" after their last child (their second son) left home to attend college in another state.

Communications training served to reduce some of the tension in the marriage, but neither spouse was willing to negotiate contingency contracts for desired changes. It was at this juncture in therapy that the Role Compromise of Central Characters technique was introduced.

Mr. Brown's favorite story was the Broadway musical *Camelot*. He identified with King Arthur whose dreams are shattered by his wife's infidelity, Guenevere's love affair with Arthur's best friend, Lancelot, "who is like a son to Arthur." Mr. Brown said that he chose Arthur as a model for identification, because "he was true to himself and his people even though it cost him dearly." He is "respected for his high principles."

Mrs. Brown's favorite book was *Gone with the Wind*. Strangely, or not so strangely, Mrs. Brown identified with Rhett Butler, "a man with a self-esteem, confidence, true to himself, strong willed" and "champion of the less fortunate." Rhett Butler also "accepted people as they are" and "did not try to change them." He is treated "with respect" because of his strong "moral principles." Rhett "walks out on Scarlet" because he "gives up trying to please her."

Obviously, this is an example of two antagonistic, conflicting and competing themes and characters. Both Mr. and Mrs. Brown believed they were "right." Mr. Brown perceived his wife's being "true to herself" as "stubbornness", and she perceived her husband's attempts to be "true to himself" as his desire "to mold her" and "to shape her" into "someone I am not."

In order to break this deadlock, Mr. and Mrs. Brown were asked to "work together on a short story" that they were "to compose themselves." The goal of the short story was to create a mutually satisfying relationship between the two characters "Rhett Butler" and "King Arthur." The setting was a "prison cell" where both had been confined together for "an indefinite time." Mr. and Mrs. Brown were asked to "figure out" how these two "strong willed" people could get along together in a way that was "mutually satisfying" and in a way that "both characters could respect each other and yet be true to themselves."

This task was one of the few assignments that the Browns were able to complete. The give and take, the negotiation and the compromise necessary to complete this joint project was a symbolic statement about what was needed in their marriage. After this assignment, the Browns viewed Rhett Butler and King Arthur differently. Both characters were still seen as strong willed, but their compassionate traits and their sense of humor were recognized.

It would be misleading and inaccurate to suggest that this brief homework assignment caused dramatic changes in the couple's characteristic way of behaving. However, it did open the door for negotiation and compromise in the marriage. The unconscious suggestion that two strong willed and independent people could get along without having to sacrifice their values and beliefs did effect the couple's ability to compromise, to some degree. However, no direct acknowledgement of this change was made by the therapist, and no further attempts to involve Mr. and Mrs. Brown in behavioral contingency contracting were made.

CONCLUSION

In this paper we have offered the reader an overview of our theoretical formulations regarding the development, maintenance and evolution of personal, conjugal and family myths. In this regard we draw heavily from a number of theoretical frameworks. Among these are family systems, human developmental, cognitive-behavioral, Jungian analytical, and object relations theories. We view the concept of myth as one way to understand: (a) the links between conscious and unconscious processes, (b) the interdependence between the individual, the family system and the broader culture, and (c) the relationships between patterned interactional behaviors and patterned perceptual processes. The symbolic aspects of myth extend far beyond the boundaries of contemporary psychological theories and touch upon the universals of human experience. Themes such as the heroic journey, the search for one's true self, primordial oneness, death, recovery from death, rebirth, renewal and the restoration of harmony link the concept of myth with the power of poetry, religious experience, drama and art.

The assessment guidelines and intervention strategies outlined in this paper and in other papers in this volume, are intended to offer rudimentary guidelines for the incorporation of a mythological perspective into one's clinical practice. However, in the final analysis, one's interest and success in implementing a mythological approach will rest more with one's own creative, right brain resources than in the suggestions offered here. We hope this volume stimulates others to experiment with their own ways of moving beyond the confines of a particular, well-accepted school of therapy and to incorporate the universal themes of human experience into their own clinical work.

NOTE

1. It is important to mention that identification with the child, projective identification and displacement also play a significant role in this process, but space and time considerations make it impossible to discuss them in any detail in this paper.

REFERENCES

Anderson, S.A. & Bagarozzi, D.A. (1983). The use of family myths as an aid to strategic therapy. *Journal of Family Therapy, 5*, 145-154.

Anderson, S.A., Bagarozzi, D.A., & Giddings, C.W. (1986). IMAGES: Preliminary scale construction. *The American Journal of Family Therapy, 14*, 357-363.

Bagarozzi, D.A. (1982, November). That was no lady, that was my wife: The role of cognitive constructs in the development of marital conflict and marital therapy. Paper presented at Department of Psychiatry, Medical College of Georgia, Augusta, GA.

Bagarozzi, D.A. (1983). Methodological developments in measuring social exchange perceptions in marital dyads (SIDCARB): A new tool for clinical assessment. In D.A. Bagarozzi, A.P. Jurich, R.W. Jackson (Eds.), *Marital and family therapy: New perspectives in theory, research and practice*. New York: Human Sciences Press, Inc.

Bagarozzi, D.A. (1983). Contingency contracting for structural and process changes in family systems. In L.A. Wolberg & M.L. Aronson (Eds.), *Group and family therapy 1982: An overview*. New York: Brunner/Mazel.

Bagarozzi, D.A. (1986). Premarital therapy. In F.P. Piercy & D. Sprenkle (Eds.), *Family therapy source book*. New York: Guilford.

Bagarozzi, D.A. & Anderson, S.A. (1982). The evolution of family mythological systems: Considerations for meaning, clinical assessment, and treatment. *The Journal of Psychoanalytic Anthropology, 5*, 71-90.

Bagarozzi, D.A. & Anderson, S.A. (in press). *Personal, marital and family myths: Theoretical formulations and clinical strategies*. New York: W.W. Norton.

Bagarozzi, D.A. & Giddings, C.W. (1984). The role of cognitive constructs and attributional processes in family therapy: Integrating intrapersonal, interpersonal and systems dynamics. In L.A. Wolberg & M.L. Aronson (Eds.), *Group and family therapy 1983: An overview*. New York: Brunner/Mazel.

Bray, J.H., Williamson, D.S., & Malone, P.E. (1984). Personal authority in the family system. Development of a questionnaire to measure personal authority in intergenerational family processes. *Journal of Marriage and Family Therapy, 10*, 167-178.

Dicks, H.V. (1967). *Marital tensions: Clinical studies toward a psychological theory of interaction*. London: Routledge and Kegan Paul.

Eliade, M. (1960). *Myths, dreams and mysteries*. London: Harvill Press.

Epstein, N., Bishop, D., & Levin, S. (1978). The McMasters model of family functioning. *Journal of Marriage and Family Counseling, 4*, 19-31.

Erikson, E. (1968). *Identity: Youth and crisis*. New York: W.W. Norton.

Feinstein, D. (1979). Personal mythology as a paradigm for a holistic public psychology. *American Journal of Orthopsychiatry, 42*, 197-217.

Lewis, J.M., Beavers, W.R., Gossett, J.T., & Phillips, V.A. (1976). *No single thread: Psychological health in family systems*. New York: Brunner/Mazel.

Minuchin, S. (1974). *Families and family therapy*. Cambridge, MA: Harvard University Press.

Olson, D.H., Portner, J., & Lavee, Y. (1985). *FACES III*. St. Paul, MN: Family Social Science, University of Minnesota.

Rogers, L.E. & Bagarozzi, D.A. (1983). An overview of relational communication and implications for therapy. In D.A. Bagarozzi, A.P. Jurich, & R.W. Jackson (Eds.), *Marital and family therapy: New perspectives in theory, research and practice*. New York: Human Sciences Press.

Sager, C.J. (1976). *Marriage contracts and couple therapy: Hidden forces in intimate relationships*. New York: Brunner/Mazel.

Sullivan, H.S. (1953). *The interpersonal theory of psychiatry*. New York: Norton.

Van Gennep, A. (1960). *The rites of passage*. Chicago: University of Chicago Press.

RESOURCE SECTION

Readers wishing to learn more about a mythological approach to therapy may find this section to be a useful starting point. Included here are summaries of key articles formerly published on the topic of family myths. Also included are selected articles which deal with intergenerational issues in family therapy. Myths and their symbolic elements are generally viewed as occurring over repeated generations in the family. Readers interested in studying family myths will also need to be familiar with how the transactional patterns that accompany symbolic, mythical themes replicate over repeated generations as well.

Annotated Bibliography
of Key Articles
on Family Myths

Gary M. Steck

Anderson, S.A. and Bagarozzi, D.A. (1983). The use of family myths as an aide to strategic therapy. *Journal of Family Therapy, 5*, 145-154.

This paper discusses how the concept of family myth can be used to organize the information generated by a family throughout the therapy process. Myth is examined in relation to mythology, the family therapy literature, and a case study. Families are seen as possessing a "shared perception of their functioning" based on nonliteral communication which a therapist interprets through the family's rituals, symbols, and metaphors. A case study is presented to illustrate the use of several strategic techniques which use the family's own symbolic language to edit the myth.

Angelo, C. (1981). The use of the metaphoric object in family therapy. *American Journal of Family Therapy, 9*, 69-78.

The author discusses the symbolic and metaphoric language of families in light of how therapists bring about change. An indepth analysis of the meaning of metaphor and metaphorical objects, both in the process between therapist and family and among family members is presented. The meaning of metaphorical objects and their therapeutic use in a communicative context is explored in several short case examples.

Gary M. Steck is a master's student in the School of Family Studies, at the University of Connecticut, U-Box 117, 843 Bolton Road, Storrs, CT 06268.

197

Bagarozzi, D.A. and Anderson, S.A. (1982). The evolution of family mythological systems: Considerations for meaning, clinical assessment, and treatment. *Journal of Psychoanalytic Anthropology*, *5*, 71-90.
This paper focuses on understanding the family context which empowers and gives foundation to a family's mythological system. The role of the family in adopting cultural/archetypal myths and in modifying these myths to fit the family's unique structure is discussed. Processes which comprise the family's mythological system, analogies, metaphors, labels, rituals, and cultural myths are assessed through the use of several guidelines. Implications for treatment include the use of role plays, enactments, and ritualized prescriptions to edit and evolve the myth toward smoother family functioning.

Byng-Hall, John (1973). Family myths used as defence in conjoint family therapy. *British Journal of Medical Psychology*, *46*, 239-250.
This key article in the development of "family myth" concept attempts to shed light on myths as a bridge between psychoanalytic and systemic theory. The formation of family mythology as a "collusive" process is discussed from the object relations and systemic perspectives. Family myths are seen as stable in that they represent an intrapsychic compromise. The function and role of family myths as part of a mythological system is addressed in case examples. Counter-transference and co-therapy are presented as issues for treatment.

Feinstein, A.D. (1979). Personal mythology as a paradigm for holistic public psychology. American *Journal of Orthopsychiatry*, *49*, 198-217.
This comprehensive work reviews the literature on cultural mythology and cognitive psychology to arrive at a definition of personal mythology as one's way of cognitively structuring reality. Personal mythology is viewed as a link between individual development and the greater social context. It is proposed that the examination of the origin and development of personal myths can enhance

individuals' sense of control and mastery in their family and the larger society. Methods to expand one's personal mythology through cognitive change are presented.

Ferreira, A.J. (1963). Family myth and homeostasis. *Archives of General Psychiatry*, *9*, 457-463.

In this paper, Ferreira builds upon the concept of "family homeostasis" to introduce the idea of "family myth." The origin and function of the family myth is discussed in light of its homeostatic effect on family interaction and family members' symptomatic behavior. Two general types of family myths, those of "happiness" and those of "unhappiness" are examined through brief case histories and subsequent therapeutic interventions.

Ferreira, A.J. (1965). Family myths: The covert rules of relationships. *International Congress of Psychotherapy*, *8*, 15-20.

The author builds upon his previous work on family myths by focusing on the covert rules and the accompanying shared beliefs and expectations among family members which comprise the family myth. The multiple roles and the complementary (reciprocal) "counter-roles" that family members play vis-à-vis one another are central elements in the family's myths. The myth explains and justifies these role arrangements. The theme of "happiness" often accompanies homeostatic family myths. Pathology is described as the presence of too many family myths, which constrict the family.

Ferreira, A.J. (1966). Family myths. *Psychiatric Research Reports*, *20*, 85-90.

In this article, Ferreira defines the term "family myth" in detail and discusses the myth as an inseparable part of the family's perceptual context. The interactional patterns under which family myths operate are described as promoting ritual. Individual roles and their complementary (reciprocal) "counter-roles" are again discussed. The origin, function and therapeutic implications of the family myth are briefly explored.

Levick, S.E., Jalali, B., and Strauss, J.J. (1981). With onions and tears: A multidimensional analysis of a counterritual. *Family Process*, *20*, 77-83.

The authors of this paper conceptualize much of the patterned behavior of disturbed families as "family rituals" and "family myths." Repetition of certain rituals is seen as perpetuating the family's mythology, and in some cases, supporting the symptoms of the identified patient. Prescribing the pathological ritual is viewed as one method to interrupt symptomatic behavior. In this paper, a counterritual is used to deflate a pathological ritual. Counterrituals are symbolic behaviors which are "anti-thetical" or oppositional to the pathological ritual.

Palazzoli, M.S., Boscolo, L., Cecchin, G.F., and Prata, G. (1977). Family rituals: A powerful tool in family therapy. *Family Process*, *16*, 445-453.

In this paper, the Milan group describes the use of prescribing a "family ritual" as a way to break a family myth which was rigidly maintained over generations without modifications. A step by step description of family therapy shows the effect of the powerful collective experience which was prescribed to explode the family myth. An indepth discussion of the meaning of ritual complements the material presented in this paper.

San Martino, M. and Newman, M.B. (1975). Intrapsychic conflict, interpersonal relationships, and family mythology. *Journal of the American Academy of Child Psychiatry*, *14*, 422-435.

The concept of family mythology is used in this article as a means of integrating the interpersonal and intrapsychic realms of family experience. The family's mythology is seen as the combination of conscious and unconscious parental fantasies which express their beliefs about relationships and human nature. Mythology is equated with the shared psychological reality of the family. Knowledge of the family's mythological system is seen as diagnostic in determining treatment and as providing the therapist with a common language for communicating with the family.

Seltzer, W.J. and Seltzer, M.R. (1983). Material, myth, and magic: A cultural approach to family therapy. *Family Process*, *22*, 3-14.

The authors of this paper present an anthropologically derived model for therapeutically approaching families as cultural systems. The authors provide a contextual guide to bringing about change in "frozen family systems" by integrating the ideas of family culture and therapeutic magic with the contemporary ideas of family ritual and myth. Therapy is seen as resembling "magic" in that it entails the manipulation of symbolically powerful material. Four case examples demonstrate the use of rituals to "unfreeze" family systems locked in stasis. The discussion of theoretical and practical implications of this approach to family therapy provides an interesting perspective for the reader.

Solomon, N. (1976). Homeostasis and family myth: An overview of the literature. *Family Therapy*, *3*, 75-86.

In this review of the literature, Solomon reviews definitions of family myth and elaborates on their homeostatic functions. The author discusses family myths as collective belief systems and elaborates their archetypical and unconscious elements. The therapeutic qualities of family myths are explored although the author makes a somewhat confusing link between myth and expectation.

Stierlin, H. (1973). Group fantasies and family myths: Some theoretical and practical aspects. *Family Process*, *12*, 111-125.

Family myths are compared to the shared fantasies that develop in small groups. As these fantasies are verbally shared, they evolve and have the power to influence group functioning. Major mythological themes, their familial functions and therapeutic implications are addressed. Myths are described as elements that bind the family together and give it a common ground. Therapists working within a family's mythological system are urged to proceed slowly, so that the myth can be gradually altered rather than dramatically extracted, therefore granting respect to the survival value a family places on its myths.

van der Hart, O. (1987). Myths and rituals: Their use in psychotherapy. In O. van der Hart (Ed.), *Coping with loss: The use of leave-taking rituals*. New York: Irvington.

This chapter of van der Hart's book compares traditional healing rituals with western therapeutic rituals. Religious healing rituals of the Navajo society and leave-taking rituals in western therapy provide the basis for this comparison. Case examples are used to illustrate: (1) the use of myth and ritual in healing; (2) how presenting symptoms are translated in terms of a therapist-created, "therapeutic myth"; (3) how the therapeutic myth is used to correct or transform the family's own myth in order to alter symptomatic behavior. Therapeutic rituals are powerful treatment tools used in conjunction with the therapeutic myth to alter family behaviors.

Warmoth, A. (1965). A note on peak experience as a personal myth. *Journal of Humanistic Psychology, 1,* 18-21.

This brief article discusses the conceptualization of "peak experience" as fulfilling the same function on an individual level that myths have historically performed for groups. Through mythology and its associated symbols, one is able to transcend a sense of self and perceive the universal themes of human experience and evolution: dependence on nature, survival, sacrifice, surrender, death-rebirth, and triumph are all symbols that embody truths that are independent of factual knowledge. The symbols of myth are described as enabling individuals to position themselves for continuation in the face of a complex of conditions that are impossible to hold in consciousness in a total, articulate framework. They serve to bring about the changes in attitude that are required by the demands and opportunities of the human condition.

Wikler, L. (1980). Folie a Famille: A family therapist's perspective. *Family Process, 19,* 257-268.

The author of this paper examines the literature on delusions shared by families. A description of families in which several members individually share identical psychotic delusions is offered. The role this disorder plays in defining functionality or dysfunctionality, and the content of these mythological systems are described in an indepth case history. An apparent underreporting of this extreme form of family myth in the literature is noted by the author.

Wolin, S.J. and Bennett, L.A. (1984). Family Rituals. *Family Process, 23*, 401-420.

Family rituals in the form of celebrations, patterned family interactions, and traditions are defined and discussed in this paper. The underlying processes of transformation, communication, and stabilization explain the powerful effects of rituals within families. Families are seen as struggling to define a suitable level of ritualization. The level of flexibility/rigidity to ritualization and the family's ability to adapt its use of ritual over time, are explored in light of assessment and treatment implications.

An Annotated Bibliography
of Intergenerational Family Issues

Stephen M. Gavazzi

I. OVERVIEW OF BASIC COMPONENTS

Boszormenyi-Nagy, I. (1986). Transgenerational solidarity: The expanding context of therapy and prevention. *The American Journal of Family Therapy*, *14*, 195-212. 374-380.

This article serves as an encapsulated version of Nagy's most recent book, *Between Give and Take* (co-authored with Barbara Krasner), which contains an update of the author's extensive work on intergenerational issues. The article addresses many critical family transactional processes, including loyalties, entitlements, reciprocity and individuation, which together form Nagy's basis for the notion of transgenerational solidarity. Much attention is given to the concept of posterity; efforts to help family members gain an awareness of the consequences of their actions across the span of many generations.

Bowen, M. (1966). The use of family therapy in clinical practice. *Comprehensive Psychiatry*, *7*, 345-374.

A seminal article which includes a comprehensive discussion of such concepts as differentiation of self, triangles, the nuclear family emotional system, the family projection process, emotional cut-offs and the multigenerational transmission process. This work will acquaint readers with the foundations from which present-day intergenerational theory and therapy has evolved.

Stephen M. Gavazzi, MA, is a PhD student in the School of Family Studies at the University of Connecticut, U-Box 117, 843 Bolton Road, Storrs, CT 06268.

Fogarty, T. (1979). The distancer and the pursuer. *The Family, 1,* 11-16.

This is a somewhat prosaic description of the evolutionary dance occurring between individuals as they seek to define relationships with each other. Relationship partners are seen as taking on different roles in which there are various degrees of comfortable or uncomfortable closeness and/or distance around relationship issues. The author notes that the clinician's greatest effectiveness in dealing with problems of closeness and distance between relationship partners or across generational boundaries often rests on creating reversals in which a former pursuer is made into a distancer and vice versa, thus altering the movement of the relationship dance.

Hoopes, M.H. (1987). Multigenerational systems: Basic assumptions. *American Journal of Family Therapy, 15,* 195-205.

The author attempts to tie together much of the theoretical, clinical and research efforts which utilize a multigenerational focus by positing eight basic assumptions thought to underlie these efforts. At first glance, this article's content may seem most valuable to the therapist gaining first exposure to multi (or inter- or trans-) generational theory and therapy. The process underlying this article, however, is valuable to the more experienced reader as well, since its attempt is to standardize and thus make explicit many ideas which often remain implicit in other writings.

Karpel, M. (1976). Individuation: From fusion to dialogue. *Family Process, 15,* 65-82.

The concept of individuation is highlighted, defined here as the process of delineating a sense of self within relational contexts. The author describes the tension which exists within this process between the dimensions of distance and relation, and describes their co-occurrence on a continuum of developmental maturity. A matrix formed from the combination of the distance and relation dimensions creates four different relationship types which are used to describe the various ways in which patterns of interaction arise between relationship partners.

Sabatelli, R.M. & Mazor, A. (1985). Differentiation, individuation and identity formation: The integration of family system and individual developmental perspectives. *Adolescence, 20*, 619-633.

The authors provide a comparison of some of the critical concepts used by intergenerational theorists, therapists and researchers. Included here is a comprehensive review of the major contributions made toward the operationalization of differentiation, individuation and identity formation, as well as a discussion of how problems are frequently encountered when these concepts are used in "overlapping and confusing ways." Building upon the major contributions reviewed, the authors assert that while these concepts are separate they are at the same time interdependent and thus provide a working integration of individual and family system issues.

Stierlin, H., Levi, L.D. & Savard, R.J. (1971). Parental perceptions of separating children. *Family Process, 10*, 411-427.

This paper combines theoretical rationale with clinical examples in order to further the understanding of the family projection process. Three areas of parental perceptions and expectations are hypothesized to exist which affect the development of offspring; specifically, these perceptions/expectations relate to (1) potential self-image and autonomy, (2) capacity to shift object relations, and (3) feelings of loyalty toward parents. The discussion of these areas in terms of their separation-inducing and/or separation-inhibiting potential lays the groundwork for Stierlin's later formulations of transactional modes (i.e., binding, delegating and expelling) which develop between the generations of families.

II. APPLICATION

Beck, R.L. (1982). Process and content in the family of origin group. *International Journal of Group Psychotherapy, 32*, 233-244.

The workings of a group that is primarily focused on family of origin material is the central component of this article. Unlike the sometimes stricter interpretation of Bowenian therapy as a secondary, almost peripheral adjunct to what is occurring in clients' personal families of origin, the author argues that the transactional modes taking place inside of the therapy group itself has a great deal of potential as an instrument of therapeutic change. The group is advocated as an ideal testing ground that allows for the understanding, preparation and practice crucial to the eventual application of what has been learned to one's family of origin.

Berger, M. & Daniels-Mohring, D. (1982). The strategic use of "Bowenian" formulations. *Journal of Strategic and Systemic Therapies, 1*, (4), 50-56.

This short article offers a slant somewhat different from most writing on clinical application of the intergenerational model since family of origin work is not usually discussed as a "strategic" form of marriage and family therapy. The authors describe various clinical situations in which intergenerational concepts are linked to strategic interventions such as reframing and paradoxical prescriptions.

Byng-Hall, J. (1980). Symptom bearer as marital distance regulator: Clinical implications. *Family Process, 4*, 355-365.

In this paper, triangulation is discussed as a process enacted by intimate relationship partners in order to resolve discomfort surrounding distance regulation issues. Once drawn into such a triangle, the recruited third party (usually a child or another family member of a different generation) is theorized to become a homeostat who consequently alleviates the couple's anxiety surrounding their fears of becoming too close and/or too distant. Through clinical examples, the author suggests that the therapist's initial task is to take over as the couple's homeostat. As the intergenerational triangulation subsides, the clinician allows distance regulation issues to emerge and be dealt with in sessions.

Hof, L. & Berman, E. (1986). The sexual genogram. *Journal of Marital and Family Therapy, 12*, 39-47.

The use of the genogram as a technique to explore the sexual dynamics of a couple and to plan therapeutic interventions is explored in this article. In a process which greatly parallels the utilization of the genogram in other areas of system functioning, the construction of the sexual genogram begins on a cognitive level by seeking information on the more "factual" aspects of the sexual histories of both partners' families of origin (i.e., who said and did what to whom). It moves with time, however, to the more emotional aspects of the couple's multigenerational experiences (i.e., uncovering partners' fears and anxieties surrounding sexual secrets and legacies in their families). Underlying the use of this assessment and intervention tool is the fact that both partners must be well-prepared, willing to participate in the process and not in the midst of a crisis situation.

Roberto, L.G. (1986). Bulimia: The transgenerational view. *Journal of Marital and Family Therapy*, *12*, 231-240.

Families with bulimic members are discussed as being organized around family legacies which emphasize the destructive aspects of success, achievement, attractiveness and the like. This author's approach to eating disorders follows a three-stage treatment plan which includes both experiential and structural as well as multigenerational components. The focus on the family as being in a situation which paradoxically provides a climate of life — as the continued survival of the family's future generations — and death — for the bulimic family member — is thought to create a context from which more constructive family legacies can emerge.

Wachtel, E. (1982). The family psyche over three generations: The genogram revisited. *Journal of Marital and Family Therapy*, *32*, 233-244.

This article notes that the original formulations about using genograms for family assessment emphasized their value in gathering the "hard facts" about family history (i.e., who did what with whom and when). Presented is a framework for going beyond this practice to include the possibility of using the genogram to uncover emotional issues and family members' idiosyncratic constructions of reality. Clinical examples are given in which myths, fantasies and the like are explored and dealt with through the utilization of what is termed a "projective" genogram.

III. INSTRUMENT DEVELOPMENT
AND RESEARCH DESIGN

Bell, L.G. & Bell, D.C. (1982). Family climate and the role of the female adolescent: Determinants of adolescent functioning. *Family Relations, 31,* 519-527.

This study explores the relationship between family climate and female adolescent functioning through the use of the Moos Family Environment Scale and a variety of individual psychological measures. Results indicate that triangulation, measured indirectly through distance scores between parents' and adolescents' answers on the Moos scale, was more likely to be present in families where an adolescent scored lower on the psychological measures, and that cross-sex coalitions (in this case between fathers and daughters) seemed more detrimental to the adolescent's psychological well-being than same-sex coalitions. Also of interest here are some exploratory indications that the role played by the triangled adolescent freed her siblings from having to perform in a similar capacity with their parents.

Bray, J.H., Williamson, D.S. & Malone, P.E. (1984). Personal authority in the family system: Development of a questionnaire to measure personal authority in intergenerational family processes. *Journal of Marital and Family Therapy, 10,* 167-178.

This scale builds on the authors' earlier theoretical formulations of a proposed "new" stage of the family life cycle — personal authority — described as the termination of the intergenerational power boundary with one's parents. The scale itself is designed to measure such variables as individuation, fusion, triangulation, intimacy and intimidation in an attempt to assess the relationship patterns which emerge across the generations of families.

Bray, J.H., Williamson, D.S. & Malone, P.E. (1986). An evaluation of an intergenerational consultation process to increase personal authority in the family system. *Family Process, 25,* 423-436.

This second paper by Bray presents initial empirical support for therapeutic efforts to enhance clients' abilities to experience personal authority in their families of origin. The researchers compared clients participating in these types of therapeutic efforts versus a control group of clients participating in system-oriented family therapy not focused on family of origin work. While the results show no differences between the groups in terms of degree of change in the presenting problem or clients' perceptions of therapeutic effectiveness, the data analysis did suggest that direct efforts to enhance personal authority were significantly more likely to positively affect such specific family processes as individuation and intergenerational triangulation.

Fleming, W.M. & Anderson, S.A. (1986). Individuation from the family of origin and personal adjustment in late adolescence. *Journal of Marital and Family Therapy, 12,* 311-315.

These researchers utilized the fusion and triangulation subscales of the Personal Authority in the Family System Questionnaire in order to explore the impact of these two intergenerational constructs on a variety of adjustment variables. The data revealed relationships between these concepts and adolescents' self-esteem and perceptions of mastery, and further evidence of a relationship between fusion and maladjustment to college and general health.

Hovestadt, A.J., Anderson, W.T., Piercy, F.P., Cochran, S.W. & Fine, M. (1985). A family of origin scale. *Journal of Marital and Family Therapy, 11,* 287-297.

These researchers were interested in assessing the perceived health of an individual's family of origin through the construction of a scale containing items related to autonomy and intimacy. This article reports on a number of previous studies utilizing this scale in which relationships were found between greater perceptions of family of origin health and such variables as positive perceptions of marriage, higher levels of rationality and greater perceptions of health in current nuclear family systems.

Teyber, E. (1983). Structural family relations: Primary dyadic alliances and adolescent adjustment. *Journal of Marital and Family Therapy, 9,* 89-99.

Adolescents' perceptions of primary relationships were explored in this study. Two main types of family structure emerged from the data analysis; adolescents reported either the parental dyad or a parent-child dyad as the most primary and important relationship in the family. Male adolescents most frequently perceived the parental dyad as primary while females most frequently perceived the mother-child relationship as the most primary. Some limited evidence suggests that female adolescents who come from families in which the parental dyad is most primary are better adjusted than those who come from families in which the parent-child relationship is primary.

Teyber, E. (1983). Effects of the parental coalitions in adolescent emancipation from the family. *Journal of Marital and Family Therapy, 9*, 305-310.

This second article by Teyber extends his previous work by exploring the effects of cross-generational versus intergenerational (parental) primary dyadic alliances. Tested and generally supported was the hypothesis that adolescents who perceive their parents' relationship as the most primary relationship in the family would have a greater ability to succeed at the developmental task of separating from parents (measured by academic success) than would those adolescents who perceive their own relationship with a parent as most primary.

IV. TRAINING AND SUPERVISION

Braverman, S. (1982). Family of origin as a training resource for family therapists. *Canadian Journal of Psychiatry, 27*, 629-633.

The utilization of family of origin material is promoted here as a method by which supervisors can help training therapists become "unstuck" and hence move beyond the various impasses created in their work with clients. By taking a survey of the training therapist's own family field, the supervisor is in a position to help the trainee identify potential similarities between what is occurring in therapeutic sessions and how current or past relationship dynamics operate in his/her own family of origin. The establishment of a sense of mutual trust and the overt willingness of the training therapist are seen as essential to the effective utilization of such material in supervisory sessions.

Guerin, P. & Fogarty, T. (1972). The family therapist's own family. *International Journal of Psychiatry, 10,* 6-50.

This article is written in two parts. The first part contains an example of a therapist incorporating intergenerational concepts in an effort to understand the workings of his own family of origin. The second part, written from the vantage point of a supervisor, consists of a description of how a training therapist's own family of origin material can shed alternative hypotheses on what is going on in training sessions. Both parts are written with frank openness and a sense of therapists' and supervisors' own vulnerabilities in dealing with their own and other's intergenerational issues.

Munson, C.E. (1984). Uses and abuses of family of origin material in family therapy supervision. *The Clinical Supervisor, 2,* 61-74.

Seeking to avoid "educational conspiracies," that is, the abandonment of certain content areas and transactional modes between supervisor and supervisee which have the potential to initiate growth and change, this paper identifies a need for a working definition of how to appropriately utilize family of origin material in supervisory sessions. Citing a lack of clinical and empirical evidence as to the effectiveness of using supervisees' personal family of origin material as the focus of supervision, and enumerating a number of harmful outcomes stemming from such a focus, the author challenges supervisors to examine the ways in which this kind of information is utilized. A number of suggestions are made which support the basic premise on which this article is written; namely, that all usages of family of origin material should be in the service of clients and not for the potential personal therapeutic benefit of the supervisee.

For Product Information and Information please contact,
our Fa representant, im OPVA@vielagsgruppe-sexon in ze., E. GmbH
Verlag GmbH, Kaufiingerstraße 24, 80331 München, German.

T - #0045 - 270225 - C0 - 212/152/12 [14] - CB - 9780866567756 - Gloss Lamination